It's Easy to Become a Citizen!

It's Easy to Become a Citizen!

★

by Carolyn Bain

HAWTHORN BOOKS, INC.

PUBLISHERS

NEW YORK

W. Clement Stone, President

323.6

CONTENTS

CHAPTER I

It's Easy to Become a Citizen

People from all over the world come to the United States to live. They come here for many reasons. One of the most important reasons is their desire to share in the freedoms that this country offers.

To enjoy these freedoms fully, most immigrants wish to become citizens. They want to be able to vote in all elections, and to be eligible for certain jobs and other benefits available only to citizens. They know that as citizens they can even run for public office and serve in any position except that of President or Vice President of the United States. An alien also looks forward to the time when, as a citizen, he will no longer be required to carry an alien registration card or to notify the Immigration and Naturalization Service of his place of residence.

This chapter tells how you, a newcomer, can become a United States citizen.

NEW WORDS YOU WILL MEET

alien: a person who lives in a country where he is not a citizen

allegiance: loyalty and devotion that a person owes to his country

application: a printed form used to request a benefit, such as naturalization

certificate: written statement of proof of some fact

clerk: one employed to keep records or accounts

Congress: the lawmaking branch of the United States Government

constitution: the fundamental law that normally governs the operation of a nation or state; (capitalized) the basic law of the United States

1

declare: to make known openly; announce formally; pronounce

democracy: government of, by, and for the people

eligible: qualified for something

examiner: one who questions another to test his knowledge

fee: money charged for services

file: to place officially on record; to submit an application for action

honorable discharge: a certificate given to a member of the Armed Forces upon completion of his satisfactory military service

immigrant: a person who has come to a new country to make his home

legal: correct according to the law

loyal: faithful to the nation; true to a friend

naturalization: the giving to a person, or the receiving by a person, of citizenship of a country other than the one in which he was born

oath: a solemn request to God to bear witness to the truth of a statement

opposed: against something

organized: put together according to law

permanent: lasting; fixed

petition: a formal written request

physically: bodily; relating to the body

preserve: save; protect; keep from harm

provisions: the terms of something, such as a law; allowance; requirements; conditions

qualification: a condition, knowledge, training, or an ability that fits a person for a particular position or work, or for a benefit such as naturalization

recommend: to offer or suggest action to be taken by another

require: demand; need

residence: place where a person lives

responsibilities: duties; obligations

spouse: husband or wife

support: uphold; be in favor of; also, keep up, pay the cost of

witnesses: persons brought before a judge or government official to tell what they have seen or know about something or someone

AN IMMIGRANT BECOMES A CITIZEN

The Congress, elected by the people of the United States, makes laws that set forth the conditions under which immigrants can become citizens. These laws assure that an immigrant can become a citizen only if he is willing to preserve and protect American democracy by fully accepting the duties and responsibilities of citizenship.

WHO CAN BECOME A NATURALIZED CITIZEN?

Congress passed the Immigration and Nationality Act in 1952. This law tells how an alien can become a naturalized citizen. In order to be eligible for naturalization under the general provisions:

He must be 18 years of age.

He must have been lawfully admitted to the United States as an immigrant, which is to say, for permanent residence.

He must have resided in this country for five years just before applying.

He must have been physically present in this country for at least a total of 30 months during this 5-year period.

He must have lived for at least the last 6 months of the 5-year period in the state in which he files his petition for naturalization.

He must be able to read, speak, understand, and write simple words in English, except that he need not satisfy these requirements if:

He is unable to speak, understand, read, or write English because of a physical disability, or

He was 50 years of age or older, and had lived in the United States for 20 years or more, on December 24, 1952.

He must have a knowledge of United States history and the United States Constitution, and understand how the government of the United States works.

He must prove that he is a person of good moral character.

He must show that he is loyal to the United States and believes in its Constitution.

He must prove that he is not and has not been opposed to organized government, and that he is not and has not been a Communist within 10 years before applying for naturalization.

A husband and wife must apply separately for naturalization. A husband's naturalization does not make his wife a citizen, nor does a wife's naturalization make her husband a citizen. However, the spouse of a citizen may apply for naturalization after 3, instead of 5, years of residence in the United States. In such a case, the applicant must also have been married to and living with his or her citizen-spouse for at least 3 years, and the spouse must have been a citizen during those 3 years.

Children born in foreign countries may become United States citizens if their parents are naturalized while the children are under 16 years of age.

Aliens who have served in the Armed Forces of the United States for 3 years may apply for citizenship while in the Armed Forces or within 6 months of honorable discharge, even though they have not lived in this country for 5 years. However, this provision of the law requires them to be lawfully permanent residents before they can apply for naturalization.

HOW TO BECOME NATURALIZED

Declaration of Intention

Before the Immigration and Nationality Act, the first step required to become a citizen was the filing of a Declaration of Intention, often called the "first papers." This is no longer a requirement of the law. However, to get certain jobs or licenses in some states, an alien may have to prove that he intends to become a citizen. If he has been lawfully admitted to the United States for permanent residence, he may do this by filing a Declaration of Intention. The necessary application is available at any office of the Immigration and Naturalization Service, or at the local naturalization court. The alien will have to complete the application and file it with the Immigration and Naturalization Service. Arrangements will then be made for him to file the Declaration of Intention with the clerk of a naturalization court. He will be required to pay a fee of $5 to the clerk of court at the time he files his declaration.

The Application to File
a Petition for Naturalization

The application to file a petition for naturalization is available at any office of the Immigration and Naturalization Service, or from the clerk of a naturalization court. When an applicant receives the application, he will also receive a fingerprint card. He may have his fingerprints taken free of charge at an office of the Immigration and Naturalization Service or at a local police station. When he has filled out the application, he should return it with the completed fingerprint card and three small photographs of himself to the Immigration and Naturalization Service office. Within a short time, he will receive a letter telling him when and where to meet a naturalization examiner who will help him file his petition for naturalization in the court. He must pay a $10 fee to the clerk of the naturalization court when he files his petition. At the time he appears to file his petition, the examiner will conduct an examination to see if he meets the legal requirements for citizenship.

The Naturalization Examination

When the applicant appears for the examination, he must have two witnesses with him who are United States citizens and who know him well. The examiner will question the witnesses about the applicant. They must be able to say truthfully that:

He is a person of good moral character.
He is loyal to the United States.
He has lived in the United States for the last 5 years.
He has been physically present in this country for at least 2½ years (30 months) of this 5-year period.
He has lived in the state where he is filing his petition for at least the last 6 months of the 5-year period.

During the examination the examiner will question the applicant to determine whether he speaks, understands, reads, and writes English; has a knowledge of United States history and government, and of the Constitution of the United States; and is otherwise eligible for naturalization.

The Final Hearing

After the petition of naturalization has been filed, it will be heard by a judge at a hearing in court. At the hearing the naturalization examiner will tell the judge of the qualifications for citizenship of each of the applicants, and will recommend whether or not each should be naturalized. The judge will decide which applicants may be given citizenship. Those who are accepted will become citizens after they take the oath of allegiance, which reads:

I hereby declare, on oath, that I absolutely and entirely renounce and abjure all allegiance and fidelity to any foreign prince, potentate, state or sovereignty, of whom or which I have heretofore been a subject or citizen; that I will support and defend the Constitution and laws of the United States of America. . . .

Each new citizen will be given a certificate of naturalization, which will entitle him to say with pride,
"I AM A UNITED STATES CITIZEN."

NOW THINK ABOUT THIS

Select from the list below the word that best completes the sentence:

permanent	fee	immigrant
Constitution	responsibilities	petition

1. All new citizens must promise to defend the _____ of the United States.

2. Each citizen of the United States has _____ as well as benefits.

3. You must have been admitted to this country for _____ residence when you apply for citizenship.

4. An alien must pay a _____ of $10 when he files his petition for naturalization.

5. Not every alien who enters the United States is an _____.

Answer briefly:

1. What must you prove in order to become naturalized?

2. How can a wife become a citizen?

3. Is a Declaration of Intention necessary in order to become a citizen?

4. What must your witnesses prove about you at your naturalization examination?

Talk about:

1. What steps must an alien take in order to become a citizen?

2. Why should an alien who is about to become a citizen be required to take an oath of allegiance?

CHAPTER 2

The Birth
of Our Nation

Since time began, people have gone from place to place in search of better ways to live.

A daring explorer, Christopher Columbus, sailed westward from Spain in 1492 looking for a new route to India. Instead of finding India, he discovered islands near the continent of North America.

The westward route discovered by Columbus opened the way to America, a new world. In the centuries that followed, millions of immigrants made the journey to this land that promised them a new way of life.

In this chapter you will learn about the early history of our country.

NEW WORDS YOU WILL MEET

assembly: a gathering of people for some purpose; meeting of lawmakers

celebrate: to recognize and honor, as a holiday

charters: official papers from a nation, or a state or city, granting certain rights and privileges and, sometimes, providing for a plan of government

colony: newly settled community that belongs to an older nation; settlement in a new land

committee: group selected to do a special job

communities: places where people live together, such as colonies, settlements, cities, or towns

continent: one of the great bodies of land in the world

created: made something new

delegate: person sent to speak or act for others, usually at meetings; to give another person the right to do this; to give authority

endowed: enriched, as with a gift; furnished; God-given; born with

establish: set up; start; found

existence: state of being; living

impressed: had a strong effect on the mind and feelings

inalienable: that which cannot be taken away

independence: freedom from control by others

liberty: freedom

limited: kept within bounds

objected: protested; opposed; was against

Parliament: British lawmaking body

possessions: land or other things that a nation or person owns and holds

privilege: right; benefit; favor

qualities: characteristics; traits

recognized: took notice of; identified; accepted

repealed: did away with (a law)

representatives: persons chosen to act for a group or groups of persons; delegates

rights: things to which one has a just claim; any benefits or privileges given to a person by law or tradition

self-government: government in which the people take part; home rule

settlement: village built by persons in a new country

treaty: formal agreement between nations

violated: broken (a law, rule, agreement, promise, etc.)

THE BIRTH OF A NEW NATION

The part of the continent of North America that became the United States was blessed with many gifts. It had vast fields of fertile soil and enough rain and sunshine to produce good crops. There were forests for wood. Wild animals and birds lived in the forests. Along the seacoasts there were natural harbors. There were many broad rivers which made boat travel easy. Streams rushing down hills and down mountainsides helped to make the work of man easier. In the earth there were valuable minerals for man to find and use.

On this continent there were people who lived in tribes. Columbus called them Indians because he thought he had reached India. They were the first Americans. Among the important American Indian tribes were the Algonquins, the Iroquois, and the Sioux. Each tribe was ruled by a chief. Like people and countries today, some of the Indians and their tribes were peaceful and some were warlike.

CHRISTOPHER COLUMBUS

Christopher Columbus, born in Genoa, Italy, was a sailor who believed the earth was round and that, by sailing westward, he would find a shorter route to India, land of spices, and other lands in Asia. He wanted to make a voyage to the west and needed money for the trip. He asked the rulers of several countries for help and, finally, Queen Isabella of Spain gave him three ships, sailors, and money for his trip. On August 3, 1492, Columbus and his men set out from Palos, Spain, in the three small ships: the *Nina,* the *Pinta,* and the *Santa Maria.*

Ten weeks later Columbus and his crew sighted land. On October 12, 1492, they landed on a small island in the Bahamas, several hundred miles southeast of what is now Florida. Still looking for the mainland of Asia, they sailed along the coasts of Cuba and Haiti. Although Columbus made three other voyages, he never found a westward route to Asia. However, he did discover a new world, America.

Every year, on October 12, the first landing of Columbus in the New World is celebrated in the Americas.

HOW AMERICA WAS NAMED

Amerigo Vespucci (1451–1512), an Italian, was one of many explorers who wrote about the discoveries in the New World. When a German mapmaker read what Vespucci had written about one of his own voyages, he was so impressed that he named the new land "America," in honor of Amerigo Vespucci.

A PERIOD OF DISCOVERY AND SETTLEMENT

A period of discovery followed the daring voyage of Columbus. Men from Spain, France, Portugal, Holland, and England traveled across the western sea, which we now call the Atlantic Ocean. Each of these explorers claimed land in the New World for his country.

Although many people came to the New World in search of adventure, others were looking for the opportunity to worship God as they pleased. Some came to America because they wanted the opportunity to earn a better living. Others had heard that there was plenty of land in the New World and that poor people could become landowners. There were also those who wanted a voice in their government and believed they would have that opportunity in the new land across the western sea.

About 750,000 people crossed the ocean to America between 1600 and 1770 to make a new and better life for themselves in the New World. A great many of these immigrants had money to pay the cost of beginning this new life. Others without money were able to come to America only by promising to work for a certain number of years for the person who paid for their travel. At the end of that time, however, they too would be able to obtain and work land of their own.

Willing hands and alert minds were needed in the New World. The newcomers were usually hard-working and daring people. Even those who had to work to pay for their travel were selected for their strength and skills. These were the qualities of the people who helped to build the United States of America.

COLONIES IN NORTH AMERICA

Many colonies were started in North America, but some of them did not succeed. To Spain belongs the honor of settling the first permanent colony in what is now the United States. This was a colony founded at St. Augustine, Florida. Other early colonists came from England. They were the next group to come in large enough numbers to form settlements that lasted. The King of England gave charters granting large areas of land in the New World to English companies and Englishmen who wished to organize groups of settlers to live and work in America.

The first successful English settlement was founded at Jamestown, Virginia, in the year 1607. In 1620 the Pilgrims, who had left England because they wanted to worship God in their own way, settled the colony of Plymouth, in Massachusetts. Other settlements were made by the Holland-Dutch in New York, the Swedes in Delaware, and the French in Louisiana. Although Pennsylvania was settled by English people, many Germans also came to live in that settlement.

For almost 70 years, both in Europe and in the American colonies, England and France fought a series of wars, broken by only short periods of peace. The last war between the French and the English colonists, which began in 1754 and ended in 1763, was called the

French and Indian War. As a result of this war, France lost almost all of her possessions in the New World to England. Other colonies in America that did not belong to England in the beginning finally came under British rule.

In 1776 there were 13 British colonies in this part of America. They were:

Connecticut	New Hampshire	Pennsylvania
Delaware	New Jersey	Rhode Island
Georgia	New York	South Carolina
Maryland	North Carolina	Virginia
Massachusetts		

These 13 colonies later became the first 13 states—the United States of America.

King George III and the Parliament in London governed the British colonies in America. However, the early charters granted by the King gave the settlers "the rights of Englishmen."

The colonists had hoped that the King and Parliament would allow them the privilege of self-government. They wanted to have assemblies to make their own laws for the protection of the lives, families, properties, and freedoms of the colonists.

The King let the colonists elect representatives to make some of the laws for their own communities. But he also sent governors from England to most of the colonies to see that English laws were obeyed. The governors collected taxes for the King on goods that the colonists brought in from other countries. Even under these conditions the colonists had a great deal of freedom and were quite content in the beginning.

After the French and Indian War, England decided to keep soldiers in the colonies. King George believed that the colonists should help to pay the cost of supporting the army. England was hard-pressed for money. The cost of the wars with France had been very high. The Parliament, to get money, passed the Stamp Act forcing the colonists to buy tax stamps for business and legal papers, as well as newspapers.

The King thought that the colonists were using goods on which taxes had not been paid. He ordered his officers to search for such goods. He even decided to tell the colonists what goods they could make, and with whom they could trade. He wanted them to trade only with the mother country, England.

All of these things angered the colonists. They stated that they could not be searched unless the officer gave them a written statement telling why the search was being made. They said that they did not like to be taxed against their wishes.

It was not that the colonists were against all taxes, for they did pay taxes on goods from other countries. However, they had no representatives in Parliament and all Englishmen believed that they could be taxed only by their own representatives. The colonists believed that is was especially unfair to force them to pay taxes when they had no such representation. They claimed that, by these taxes, their rights as Englishmen were not being respected.

King George and Parliament at first refused to change the tax laws. Nevertheless, many people in the colonies would not buy the tax stamps and some colonists took the stamps and burned them. Within a year, friends of the colonists in Parliament were able to get the Stamp Act repealed.

A tax was then placed on all paint, paper, glass, lead, and tea brought into the colonies. The colonists once again objected to the new taxes and refused to buy these goods from England. As a result of their refusal to buy English goods, the King and Parliament finally agreed to repeal all of the taxes except the one on tea. The King kept this tax because he felt that there must always be at least one tax in force to show that he could tax the colonists.

In 1773 the British East India Company shipped millions of pounds of tea to the colonies. The colonists would not permit the tea to be removed from the ships. Several ships returned to England. In Boston, Massachusetts, the colonists boarded the ships and threw the tea into the harbor. This was called the Boston Tea Party. Parliament then passed acts that closed the port of Boston and limited the freedom of the colonists.

THE COLONISTS MEET

The colonists decided to meet to discuss the troubles they were having with England. They elected representatives who met in Philadelphia in the autumn of 1774. It was the First Continental Congress. All of the colonies, except Georgia, sent representatives to the meeting. The Congress sent a petition to King George asking him to respect the rights of the colonists. The King and Parliament refused.

The Second Continental Congress, made up of delegates from all 13 colonies, first met in Philadelphia on May 10, 1775. This Congress elected George Washington as commander in chief of the Continental Army and the colonists went to war against England.

DECLARATION OF INDEPENDENCE

Even though the colonists were at war with England, many of them hoped to remain British subjects. They believed that King George would change his mind about the new laws when he saw how determined they were to oppose them. The King decided to be even more firm and, to make matters worse, he hired German soldiers to fight the colonists in America.

More and more of the colonists and their leaders spoke of complete separation from Great Britain. One of the strongest arguments for independence came from the pen of Thomas Paine. In his pamphlet *Common Sense*, he said that Americans had a natural right to their own government and called upon the people to break away from the mother country.

During the Second Continental Congress, Richard Henry Lee of Virginia made this motion, "Resolved: That these United Colonies are, and of right ought to be, free and independent states."

This motion was discussed by the delegates and a committee was appointed to write a Declaration of Independence.

Thomas Jefferson, a leading member of the committee, did most of the writing. On July 4, 1776, the Declaration of Independence was accepted by the Second Continental Congress, although it was not signed by all delegates until almost a month later.

The Declaration of Independence set forth ideas that were new to most people. It declared that all men are created equal, and that they are endowed by their Creator with certain inalienable rights, among which are life, liberty, and the pursuit of happiness. The Declaration also stated that governments are established to protect the rights of the people and that laws should not be made unless the people agree to them. It further stated that when a government makes laws without their agreement, the people have every right to establish a new government. The Declaration listed the rights of the colonists which the King and the Parliament had violated and declared that the colonies were then separating from Great Britain and were free from all British control.

When the Second Continental Congress asked a committee to draw up a statement of independence, it recognized the independence already in existence in the colonies. The Declaration of Independence announced to the world the separation and independence of the colonies from Great Britain. The 13 colonies became the first 13 states. The United States of America was born!

THE REVOLUTIONARY WAR

King George was angered by the Declaration of Independence and decided that Great Britain would continue to fight to keep the colonies.

The King's soldiers had good clothes and food, and were well trained. The American army under Washington was untrained. The men were poorly clothed and they used old guns. They did not always have enough food. Some of the soldiers had borrowed money so that their families could live while they were away at war. Other men wanted to go home to raise food for their families. General Washington tried in every way to get food, clothes, guns, and ammunition for his soldiers, but he was not very successful.

Meanwhile, the King had trouble at home after the decision was made to fight to hold the colonies. Great Britain found herself at war with both Spain and France. At this time France also decided to send help to the colonists.

The Revolutionary War, also called the War for Independence, was a long and hard war. Freedom-loving people from many countries came to help the colonists. Lafayette, Rochambeau, and the German-born De Kalb came from France; Pulaski and Kosciusko from Poland; and Von Steuben from Germany. These men helped George Washington train and lead the American soldiers. In 1781 Washington, with the help of Lafayette, surrounded the British at Yorktown, Virginia. The French Navy joined in the fight at Yorktown against the British warships. After several weeks of fighting, the British commander, Lord Cornwallis, surrendered. This ended the actual war, but it was not until two years later that a peace treaty was signed between Great Britain and the new United States. By this treaty, the British recognized the United States as an independent nation.

INDEPENDENCE DAY

In our American history July 4, 1776, marks the birth of the United States of America. The Fourth of July, Independence Day, is a national holiday. All the people in the United States celebrate this day.

NOW THINK ABOUT THIS

In the list below find the word or words that can take the place of the underlined words in the sentences:

established	1. Parliament did away with some tax laws.
privilege	2. The colonists protested the Stamp Act.
repealed	3. The American colonists fought for their freedom.
endowed	4. Many colonies were set up in the New World.
objected to	5. The colonists wanted the right of self-government.
independence	6. The Declaration of Independence said that people were born with certain rights.

In the left column are the names of persons you have met in the chapter. Match each name with the words in the right-hand column that tell who the person was:

1. Thomas Paine	led the Continental Army.
2. Amerigo Vespucci	wrote the pamphlet *Common Sense*.
3. Christopher Columbus	was the French leader who aided George Washington.
4. King George	wrote most of the Declaration of Independence.
5. Lafayette	wrote about his trips to the New World which was later named for him.
6. George Washington	landed in America in 1492.
7. Thomas Jefferson	taxed the colonies.

From the following list select the correct word(s) to complete each sentence:

Parliament	George Washington
Continental Congress	Pilgrims
thirteen (13)	Fourth of July

Declaration of Independence

1. There were _____ colonies in America in 1776.
2. The _____ settled in Massachusetts.
3. The lawmaking body in England is called the _____.
4. We celebrate our nation's birthday on the _____.
5. The Continental Congress elected _____ to lead the army against the British.

6. The written statement sent to the King stating the rights of colonists was called the_____.

7. The representatives who met to protect the rights of the people were called the _____.

Talk about:

1. Why was Columbus' discovery so important?

2. What is meant by the statement in the Declaration that "all men are created equal"?

CHAPTER 3

Planning a New Government for a New Nation

Before the Revolutionary War, the British thought that the American colonies could not develop great statesmen who would be able to work with the statesmen of other governments. Great Britain forgot that struggles for freedom produce great leaders. Men such as Washington, Jefferson, and Franklin led the colonists in their struggle for independence, and they became great leaders and statesmen.

War affects all the people of a nation. The Revolutionary War increased the demand for guns, ammunition, clothing, food, and other supplies. There was an increase in iron, steel, and textile production. Spinning wheels hummed in newly formed spinning clubs in towns and villages. Looms clattered, turning out more and more woolen, linen, and cotton cloth for uniforms and clothing. Great Britain had sold these goods to the colonies before the war. The young states were now gaining a new kind of independence by producing their own materials.

Throughout the war, patriotic women in the colonies were at work in many ways. They were active in making ammunition, in spying, and in aiding the fighting men. Some women farmed while their husbands and sons were on the battlefields. One English officer complained to his general that, if their army destroyed all the men in America, they still would have to conquer the women before the war would be won.

The people showed an interest in many new things at this time. They were interested in current events and politics, and they especially wanted to know about their local government. Their demand for daily news about the progress of the war led to an increase in the number of newspapers.

In these many ways the young United States was becoming fully independent of the mother country. But, although a new nation had been born, troubles were ahead.

In this chapter you will read about how the United States became a republic, a form of democracy.

NEW WORDS YOU WILL MEET

adopted: accepted

affect: act upon or influence; change in some way

appointed: assigned, or named, to an office

approval: acceptance; ratification

authority: power or right to act or command

checks and balances: a system whereby each branch of government has some control over the other branches

coin: make into money by stamping metal; metal money

commerce: trade between persons or groups of persons, or states, or nations

convention: a meeting for some purpose

debates: arguments about issues; discussions of any questions

defense: protection from others; providing protection for all the people, as expressed in the Constitution

document: an official paper; also, a paper relied upon to prove some fact

enforce: to compel obedience (to a law)

executive: having to do with enforcing the laws; also, the person or branch that enforces the laws

express: make clear by acts or words

finance: the system by which money is raised and spent

function: to operate or work; the operation or work called for; the purpose or use of something

influence: power to change; ability to bring about a result; pressure

judicial: having to do with courts and judges and explaining the laws; also, the branch of government which explains the laws

legislative: having to do with lawmaking; also, branch of government which makes the laws

levy: to place a tax on something

objectives: purposes; results to be realized; goals

posterity: people who will live in the future; future generations

power: authority to control; influence; strength or force

purpose: the object or result aimed at; the reason for doing something

ratified: accepted and made official; approved
regulate: make rules for something; govern according to rule
republic: a nation having a representative form of government
revolution: an overthrow of the government by the governed
supreme: highest in rank; highest in authority and importance
trade: buying and selling goods; commerce
tranquility: condition of being calm, peaceful, or quiet
  veto: refuse to allow a bill to become a law by not signing it; refuse
to approve; disapprove
  wisdom: knowledge and good judgment based on experience; being
wise

PLANNING A NEW GOVERNMENT FOR A NEW NATION

THE ARTICLES OF CONFEDERATION

During the Revolution, the members of the Second Continental Congress continued to hold meetings and to serve in the central government of the colonies. The Congress wanted to establish a simple framework of government for the colonies, which were soon to become states with the adoption of the Declaration of Independence. It appointed a committee in June 1776 to write a plan of confederation for the states. The committee called its plan "The Articles of Confederation." This plan was adopted by the Congress in 1777 and was sent to the states to be ratified by them. When the state of Maryland finally gave its approval in 1781, the Articles of Confederation went into effect.

The Articles of Confederation provided that the states were entering into a "firm league of friendship" and a "perpetual union for the common defense, the security of their liberties, and their mutual and general welfare." A Congress, made up of representatives from the 13 states, was to be the central government for the new United States under the Articles of Confederation.

This was the first step toward a republic.

WHAT FREEDOM BROUGHT

The new freedom of the states from Great Britain brought many changes and new responsibilities which had to be met by the Congress of the new Confederation.

No longer were there 13 colonies; there were 13 states.

No longer was there a single purpose—the fight for independence that united the states; new purposes were needed to keep them united.

No longer would the 13 colonies be protected by Great Britain; the states would have to protect themselves.

No longer would Great Britain control the trade of the colonies; the states would have to control their own trade.

No longer would money from Great Britain be used; the states would have to coin their own money.

The 13 struggling states, like young children without their mother, began to quarrel. Each state started to run its local government for its own good, rather than for the good of the whole nation.

The Articles of Confederation did not give enough power to the central government.

There was no executive officer to enforce the laws.

The Congress could levy taxes by asking the states for money, but it had no power to make the states pay the money.

The Congress could not control trade between the states.

The Congress had no good way to settle quarrels among the states.

A CRITICAL TIME IN AMERICAN HISTORY

Because of the weaknesses of the Articles of Confederation, the states began to drift apart and to distrust one another. As a result, some of the leading men of the states argued that there must be a stronger central government with enough authority to force the states to obey its laws. It was difficult to get started on such a plan of action. The Congress, the only central group representing the 13 states, finally suggested that the states arrange for a convention to change and strengthen the Articles of Confederation.

THE CONSTITUTIONAL CONVENTION OF 1787

The Constitutional Convention began its meetings in Independence Hall in Philadelphia on May 25, 1787. This was the same hall in which the Declaration of Independence had been signed almost 11 years earlier. The state governments had named more than 70 delegates to attend the convention, but only 55 actually attended. The convention soon decided that the Articles of Confederation could no longer serve as a framework for the government of the new United States, and that a new constitution would have to be written.

GREAT MEN LEAD THE CONVENTION

In 1787 the states sent some of their most able leaders to the Constitutional Convention in Philadelphia. These great men created one of the most famous and respected documents in the world, the Constitution of the United States. Among the great leaders were:

George Washington, who served as President of the convention through its long meetings. His wisdom and influence guided the delegates and held them together.

Benjamin Franklin, the elderly delegate from Pennsylvania, whose personality and good advice helped to keep the convention running smoothly.

James Madison, a Virginian who knew a great deal about governments and constitutional law. He is said to have written most of the Constitution with the able help of Gouverneur Morris, James Wilson, and Alexander Hamilton.

Alexander Hamilton, of New York, who was a student of finance and government. Although Hamilton opposed some of the ideas and provisions of the Constitution, he worked almost without sleep to have it adopted.

James Wilson, who was sent by Pennsylvania to the convention, was an authority in political and legal matters.

Gouverneur Morris, from Pennsylvania, who became responsible for the final wording of the Constitution because of his keen mind and ability to write.

These men and the other 49 delegates decided that everything which had been said and written at the convention should be kept secret until the Constitution was completed. Each delegate tried to represent the wishes of the people who had sent him to the convention and, at the same time, work for the good of all the people. All through the hot summer there were stormy debates, but these wise men learned to compromise. Each delegate, at times, gave up something he wanted in order to reach an agreement that would help the whole country.

THE OBJECTIVES OF THE CONSTITUTION

The Preamble to the Constitution, in 52 words, stated the purposes and objectives of the new union of the states under the Constitution. The passing years have created many new needs which, in turn, have required changes to be made in the law. The writers of the Constitution provided a way in which these changes could be made. Such changes are called amendments. However, the purposes of our Constitution and the government it established have not changed.

Constitution of the United States of America

Preamble

We the People of the United States, in order to form a more perfect Union, establish justice, insure domestic tranquility, provide for the common defense, promote the general welfare, and secure the blessings of liberty to ourselves and our posterity, do ordain and establish this Constitution for the United States of America.

In these first words, the Preamble to the Constitution clearly states that the supreme power of government is in the hands of "We the People." Nearly every word in this opening paragraph of the Constitution expresses an important idea. It is well worth studying.

SOME OLD IDEAS OF GOVERNMENT HONORED

In order to carry out the purposes and reach the objectives set forth in the Preamble, the delegates to the convention studied the plans of government used in England, in the former colonies, and in the states. The best ideas from each of these plans they wrote into the new Constitution.

NEW IDEAS OF GOVERNMENT ALSO ADDED

The delegates also found it necessary to write into the Constitution certain new ideas of government to assure that the aims and goals set forth in the Preamble would be reached.

The new Constitution provided for three branches of government:

The legislative branch, called Congress, which makes the laws;

The executive branch, headed by a President, which enforces the laws; and

The judicial branch, which is the system of courts and judges, that explains the laws.

The Constitution provided that the legislative branch would have two Houses, the House of Representatives and the Senate. Members of the House of Representatives were to be elected according to population. As a result, a state with more people would have more members in this House than would a state with fewer people, and it would, therefore, have greater power. In the Senate each state would have two Senators, and, therefore, each state would have equal power. Each House, however, would have equal rights in making the laws.

The new Congress would have authority to make laws governing all matters of national interest. It would have power to levy and collect taxes, regulate interstate and foreign commerce, spend money for common defense, and spend money for the general welfare. These were matters which would be of interest to all the states as a nation.

Each of the young 13 states would have to share much of its power with the new United States of America.

CHECKS AND BALANCES IN THE CONSTITUTION

The delegates created a Constitution which was strong enough to bind the states together as a nation but which also left power in the hands of the people.

By dividing power among three branches of government, no one branch could control the government.

By having two Houses in Congress, no single group could make the laws.

By having the members of the House of Representatives elected according to the population of a state, the larger states would have more power in the House.

By having two Senators elected from each state, each state would have equal representation and power in the Senate.

By having a President with power to veto laws of Congress, unwise laws would be sent back to Congress to be studied again.

By creating the Supreme Court with final authority in law, the will of one high court would be final, rather than the clashing wills of the 13 states.

These are some of the checks and balances which were carefully written into the Constitution.

SIGNING AND RATIFYING THE CONSTITUTION

Their work finally completed, on September 17, 1787, the delegates signed the Constitution. Of the 55 delegates attending the convention, only 39 actually signed the Constitution. It then had to be sent to the 13 states to be ratified. Approval by nine states was necessary before it would become the law of the land.

Before the end of June 1788, nine states had ratified the Constitution. Some states felt that it was incomplete because it did not provide for all the rights and freedoms of individuals. When these states were promised that the Constitution would be amended to add these rights, they accepted the document. The two large states of Virginia and New York at first were undecided. By the end of July 1788, however, these states approved the Constitution. North Carolina ratified it in November 1789, and Rhode Island followed with its approval in the spring of 1790.

The United States of America began to function under the Constitution in 1789. It was the first country in the world that began life with a written Constitution assuring freedom to each of its citizens.

NOW THINK ABOUT THIS

Select the word from Column B that you can associate with the word from Column A:

Column A	Column B
1. ratified	a. taxes
2. document	b. trade
3. judicial	c. approved
4. commerce	d. courts
5. checks	e. Constitution
6. levy	f. balances

Answer briefly:
1. What was the first step the colonists took toward a republic?
2. Why did the states begin to quarrel with each other?
3. What was the purpose of the Constitutional Convention?
4. Name three great leaders who attended the convention.
5. What are the three branches of our government?
6. What is the purpose of the checks and balances that are written into the Constitution?
7. What does the Constitution assure to each American citizen?

Talk about:
1. The purpose of the Preamble to the Constitution of the United states.
2. Why must people sometimes compromise with what they want?

CHAPTER 4

Giving Government the Power to Work

The year was 1619. The place was Jamestown, Virginia, the first permanent English settlement in America. Twenty-two men, two elected by the people of each of Virginia's 11 boroughs, met in an assembly called the House of Burgesses. These delegates met to make laws for all the people of Virginia. Representative government had begun in America.

A year later a meeting much like the one at Jamestown was held aboard a little ship named the *Mayflower,* which brought the Pilgrims to America. The leaders of this little band of Pilgrims had asked all the men aboard the ship to help frame an agreement stating how the new colony at Plymouth would be governed. The agreement, called the Mayflower Compact, said that the men would make and obey "just and equal laws" for the good of their colony.

As shown here, self-government was part of the very beginning of English settlement in the New World.

In this chapter you will learn how our representative government received its power to delegate authority.

NEW WORDS YOU WILL MEET

ballot: a system of secret voting by the use of a printed form or a machine; the printed form itself

basically: fundamentally; of first importance

boroughs: towns smaller than cities; also, divisions within larger cities

26

concerned: interested in; related to; was about something

delegated authority: power or right to act for another person or persons

efficiency: the way to get the best results with the least cost of time, money, and effort

indicated: pointed out; showed

mayor: chief executive of a city government

prohibited: forbidden; not allowed

GIVING GOVERNMENT THE POWER TO WORK

As was the case with the Pilgrims, the laws in early America were made by all the men who were to obey the laws. As the number of people increased, it became impossible for all persons concerned with government to meet to make laws. Thus, when the colony in Virginia had grown to 11 boroughs, men had to be chosen by their neighbors to represent them in the House of Burgesses. Each man chosen was called a representative. When the population of the colony increased, each man in the House simply represented more colonists.

Choosing a representative is done by voting. When there are few voters, voting many be done by a show of hands. When the number of people voting is so large that all of them cannot meet in one room, written votes are usually cast at public places, called polls. The form on which the vote is recorded is called a ballot. Most voting in the United States is done by ballot. However, where the number of voters is very large, a voting machine may be used for recording votes.

Suppose that, in a recent election for Senator, people had a choice of voting for Tom Wells or Burt Hay. When the votes were counted, Wells had received 8,000 votes and Hay had received 10,000. This, of course, would indicate that the people had elected Burt Hay as Senator.

Until the next election for Senator, Mr. Hay's decisions as Senator will be the decisions of all the people he represents. When Mr. Hay's six-year term in the Senate is over, the people will probably reelect him if they think he has done what they wanted done. If Mr. Hay has not carried out the wishes of the voters, they can, and probably will, elect a new Senator.

FINAL AUTHORITY

In a democracy, such as our republic, final authority in government rests with the people.

Because the people have the power to choose their representatives, they will always have the final power in governing themselves.

DELEGATED AUTHORITY

Often the word "authority" is used to mean power. Authority in government, under our democracy, means the power to act for the people. Such authority was given at Jamestown in 1619 when the voters gave their delegates power to act for them. This is called delegated authority.

A good example of delegated authority is that received by the mayor of a city. Among his duties is the protection of people and their property, and authority is given to him by the people to do whatever must be done to perform that duty. The mayor, in turn, delegates his authority to a chief of police who then has power to take action to assure that the police force does its work well and protects the people and their property. Should the police force not do its work properly, the mayor will call upon the police chief to explain why something was done, or was not done. Should the matter be serious enough, the mayor may even delegate his authority to a new chief of police. The mayor can delegate his authority, but not his responsibility. He will always be basically responsible for the efficiency of the police force in protecting the people and their property. If he has not properly used the authority delegated to him, the people will delegate their authority to a new mayor at the next election.

Authority delegated by the people can always be taken away by the people.

The men who drew up the Constitution of the United States did not have the power to tell the people to accept the Constitution. Therefore, it was presented to the people in each state so that they might vote for or against its approval. In turn, the people selected representatives to meet in state conventions for the purpose of deciding by vote whether or not the new plan of government should be accepted. The final power to accept the Constitution thus remained with the people of the United States.

DELEGATED AUTHORITY
IN FEDERAL GOVERNMENT

The Federal government is another name for the government of the nation. The Federal government receives its basic power to govern from authority delegated to it in the Constitution and its amendments. When Congress, the President, or a Federal court takes action, each must do so under and within the limits of delegated authority.

However, as stated earlier, authority delegated by the people can be taken away by the people. The 18th amendment to our Constitution prohibited the manufacture of, and trade in, intoxicating liquors and delegated authority to the Congress and the states to pass laws enforcing the amendment. This delegated authority was taken away from the Congress by the 21st amendment, which repealed the 18th amendment.

We have seen that the people of all the states, through the Federal Constitution, delegated to a Federal government the powers needed to govern the nation. Powers of government not delegated in this manner remained with the people of the several states.

The people of each state adopted a constitution which provides a general plan of government for the state. The constitution of each state declares that the final authority in state government belongs to the people of that state. However, the state government, through the people, has only those powers not delegated to the Federal government.

Each state constitution makes provision for the same three branches of government as those of the Federal government. The people have delegated to an executive branch the authority to enforce the state laws. To a legislative branch has been delegated the authority to make state laws. To the state courts the people have delegated the authority to decide questions about the state law.

Just as the Federal Constitution provides a method by which it may be amended, each state constitution also indicates how it may be changed. For example, an important change in a state constitution took place in Nebraska. The constitution of this state had at one time divided the lawmaking branch into two legislative houses. Later, the people of Nebraska decided that one house would be better. They amended the state constitution to provide that the lawmaking branch should consist of only one legislative body. The constitution of every state can be amended to bring about changes in the state government in accordance with the wishes of the people.

DELEGATED AUTHORITY IN CITIES AND TOWNS

The government of a state has the authority to govern its people, but only because they have delegated that power to it in a state constitution. The state government cannot govern the people properly unless a plan of government is provided for smaller communities within the state, such as cities and towns. The state government grants charters to the cities and towns for that purpose. In these charters the state government delegates to the communities a part of the authority to govern which it received from the people. Under such a charter, a community has the power to make local laws. Since the community's authority to make local laws is delegated by the state government, it cannot be greater than the authority of the state government. Consequently, the local laws passed by a community must agree with the constitution and laws of the state. Furthermore, since the state government received its power to govern from the people, it can be seen that the final authority in city and town governments also belongs to the people.

GOVERNMENT POWER IS DELEGATED AUTHORITY

All government in the United States—Federal, state, and local—is government of the people, not one class or one group of people but *all* of the people; by the people, because the people elect the officers who carry on the work of the government; for the pople, because the government is planned for the good of all the people.

NOW THINK ABOUT THIS

Select from the list below the word that best completes each sentence:

mayor	reelect	provide
prohibit	delegated	basically

1. If a representative accomplishes what the people want done, they will probably _____ him.
2. The Federal government may _____ the levying of certain taxes by the states.
3. The mayor is _____ responsible for good government in his city.
4. State constitutions also _____ for a method of amendment.

5. Authority _____ by the people may be taken away by the people.

Answer briefly:
1. What is a ballot?
2. What is meant by delegated authority?
3. What are the branches of state government?
4. Who has final authority in a state?
5. How does a state delegate authority to local communities?

Talk about:
1. Why do our citizens choose representatives?
2. What do we mean when we say that all government in the United States is government of, by, and for the people?

CHAPTER 5

Creating the New Government and the Bill of Rights

The Constitution grows in different ways. One way it grows is through decisions of the Federal courts. The decisions explain provisions that are not entirely clear and give to them their full meaning.

The Constitution also grows by amendment. The first big growth took place with the addition of the first ten amendments. Each one of these amendments protects one or more of the rights of the people and they are, therefore, called the Bill of Rights. You will read about the Bill of Rights in this chapter.

NEW WORDS YOU WILL MEET

accused: charged a person with wrongdoing; also, the person so charged

administered: directed the taking of (the oath of office); carried out

civil case: a lawsuit, not involving a crime, brought by or against a person, state, or nation (see criminal case) (explained in detail in chapter 9)

contained: included; was a part of

crime: an act which is against the law; an unlawful act

criminal case: a lawsuit brought by the state or nation against a person accused of having committed a crime (see civil case) (explained in detail in chapter 9)

electors: persons chosen by the voters for the purpose of electing the President and Vice President

excessive: too large; beyond any degree or limit; extreme

guarantees: promises; assurances given that something would be done

inauguration: ceremony when President is sworn into office

included: was among; formed a part of something

involves: has to do with; concerns; includes

jury: a group of citizens who are chosen to listen to trials in a court and decide which side is right

legislature: lawmaking body

quartering: assignment of housing, as for soldiers

reserved: saved, especially for a purpose

testify: make a statement under oath in order to prove that something is true

trial: hearing in a court of justice; judicial hearing

warrant: a legal document giving authority to do something

CREATING THE NEW GOVERNMENT AND THE BILL OF RIGHTS

After the Constitution had been accepted, its plan of government had to be put into effect. The first step in this direction was the election of a President and a new Congress. The Constitution stated how the members of the two Houses of Congress and a President should be chosen. It provided that the people of each state should elect persons to represent them in the House of Representatives, and that each state legislature should elect two Senators to the Senate. It also provided that the people should vote for electors, who would then vote for two persons—one to be President and one to be Vice President.

THE FIRST ELECTION

The people of the states voted for the electors who thereafter gathered and cast their votes for the President and the Vice President. George Washington received the vote of every elector. To date he has been the only President so honored. John Adams, having received the next highest number of votes, became Vice President.

GEORGE WASHINGTON INAUGURATED
APRIL 30, 1789

George Washington had no desire to be President. After the war he wanted to live quietly at his home in Mount Vernon, Virginia. But his country wanted him to serve again—and needed him—so he accepted the responsibility of President of the new United States. On April 16, 1789, he left his home and went to New York City, at that time the capital of the nation. It was a long journey on horseback.

Washington's journey to New York must have made him happy— the towns through which he passed gave great dinners in his honor; roads were lined with cheering crowds; children sang for him; guns in the villages were fired when he arrived, and again when he left.

He was met at the New Jersey coast by a large boat that had been sent from New York. It was hung with red and white bunting and was rowed by ship captains who were dressed in white. The guns of all the ships in the harbor sounded their welcome to the first President of the United States as the boat crossed the harbor to the city.

A new Congress had also been elected. It was to have met for the inauguration of the President on the 4th of March in 1789. Travel in those days was slow, however, and some of the members of Congress were late in arriving in New York City. It was late in April before everything was ready for the inauguration.

The inauguration took place on the last day of April in Federal Hall. Robert Livingston, Chancellor of the State of New York, administered the oath of the office of President which the Constitution requires every President to take. George Washington, his hand on an open Bible, spoke the following words:

I do solemnly swear that I will faithfully execute the office of President of the United States, and will to the best of my ability, preserve, protect and defend the Constitution of the United States.

The Bible was raised and Washington kissed it as the seal of his pledge.

On April 30, 1789, the United States of America had its first President under the Constitution. The government provided for by the Constitution became a living government.

THE PRESIDENT AND THE CONGRESS BEGIN THEIR WORK

The first work of the President and the new Congress was to organize the government which was so carefully planned by the writers of the Constitution.

Congress began its work by passing a law that provided for executive departments to assist and advise the President. To head these departments, the President appointed Alexander Hamilton as Secretary of the Treasury, Thomas Jefferson as Secretary of State, and Henry Knox as Secretary of War. The offices of Attorney General and Postmaster General were also created. To these positions the President appointed Edmund Randolph as Attorney General, and Samuel Osgood as Postmaster General. These men soon came to be known as the President's Cabinet, although there was no provision in the law for a Cabinet until over a hundred years had passed.

Congress also passed a law organizing the Federal courts. The President appointed the judges and, as required by the Constitution, the Senate approved the appointments.

Congress placed a tax on goods brought into the United States from other countries. This tax money helped to pay expenses of the new government.

THE CONGRESS HAS A PROBLEM

Some of the states had ratified the Constitution only when they were promised that a Bill of Rights would be added to it. State constitutions already contained such provisions, and many state leaders felt that the Federal Constitution should also guarantee in writing the rights and freedoms of the people.

When the new Congress met, some of its members thought that there should be no hurry to amend the Federal Constitution. However, James Madison, now elected to the House of Representatives, and other members of the Congress spoke out in favor of adding the amendments immediately.

After much discussion, 12 amendments were approved by Congress and were sent to the states for acceptance. By 1791 ten of them were ratified and became law. These amendments were written into the Constitution as the Bill of Rights. Not only were the people free, but they had a Constitution which included a Bill of Rights that guaranteed their freedom.

You will want to read every word of the first ten amendments to the Constitution. They are:

Amendment 1—Freedom of Religion, of Speech, and of the Press; Right to Assemble and Right of Petition
Guarantees freedom of religion, freedom of speech, and freedom of the press.

Guarantees the right to assemble peaceably, and the right to ask the government to change the laws.

Amendment 2—Right to Keep Arms

Gives the people the right to have weapons.

Amendment 3—Quartering of Soldiers

Provides that, in time of peace, no soldiers shall be placed in a private home without the approval of the owners.

Amendment 4—Warrants of Search and Seizure

Assures that there shall be no search or seizure of persons or things without the legal authority of a warrant, properly issued, setting forth the cause, and describing the person or place to be searched or the person(s) or thing(s) to be seized.

Amendment 5—Guarantees in Criminal Cases; Fair Price for Property

Guarantees that no person can be held to answer (brought to trial) for a serious crime without first having been accused by a Grand Jury, except persons actually in military service in time of war or public danger. (Members of the Armed Forces are tried by a military court without action by a Grand Jury.)

No person can be tried twice for the same crime.

No person in any criminal case shall have to testify against himself.

Life, liberty, or a person's property shall not be taken from him without a court trial. Property will not be taken for public use without a fair price being paid for it.

Amendment 6—Rights of Accused Persons

Guarantees an accused person the right to a trial by jury.

Provides that a person accused of a crime must be told plainly the nature of the crime of which he is accused.

He has the right to have a lawyer to defend him.

An accused person has the right to hear and question those who say he has committed a crime.

All witnesses who testify against an accused person must do so in his presence.

He has the right to compel any person to appear in court as a witness to testify in his favor.

Amendment 7—Trial by Jury in Civil Cases

States that a trial by jury is guaranteed in any lawsuit which involves a claim of more than $20.

Amendment 8—Excessive Punishments

Prohibits excessive bail, excessive fines, and cruel and unusual punishments.

Amendment 9—Rights Reserved to the People
Declares that rights which the people may have had before the adoption of the Constitution are not taken away, nor do they have any lesser value, because they are not mentioned in the Constitution.
Amendment 10—Powers Reserved to the States
Declares that any powers not given to the Federal government, nor clearly taken away from the states, are reserved to the states, or to the people.

NOW THINK ABOUT THIS

Use each of the following phrases in a sentence of your own:
1. an accused person
2. a search warrant
3. administered the oath
4. witnesses for the accused
5. reserved to the states
6. contained in the Bill of Rights
7. a jury in civil cases

Answer these questions:
1. When was George Washington inaugurated?
2. How was Washington honored on his trip to New York City?
3. Who were the members of Washington's Cabinet?
4. What are the first ten amendments to the Constitution called?

After each of the statements below the boxes, write in the number of the amendment in which the statement can be found:

Amendment I	Amendment 5	Amendment 6	Amendment 8
Freedom of Religion, of Speech, and of the Press	Criminal Cases	Rights of Accused Persons	Excessive Punishments

A person cannot be forced to testify against himself. _____
Citizens have the right to assemble peaceably. _____
An accused person has the right to have a lawyer. _____

An accused person cannot be required to post excessive bail._____
No person can be tried twice for certain crimes. _____
The government cannot take property without paying a fair price
    for it. _____
A person can go to the church of his own choosing. _____

Talk about:
Why is the Bill of Rights important to every American citizen?

CHAPTER 6

Congress—The Legislative Branch of Our Government

You will recall that the Federal Constitution was drawn up to provide only the broad outlines of the nation's government. No attempt was made to include in that document a complete and detailed description of the entire structure and operation of the government. Using foresight, the authors of the Constitution left many details of such matters to be developed over a period of time by the future government. They wisely reasoned that the persons elected to conduct the business of government would be in the best position to determine the exact machinery and procedures needed for this purpose.

The way in which Congress works and the legislative tools that it has created illustrate what has been said above, as we will see. The Constitution provides for a Congress, consisting of the Senate and the House of Representatives, to make laws for the nation. It lists the qualifications of Senators and Representatives, states how they are to be elected, and grants them authority to pass laws concerning certain matters.

The Constitution, however, does not describe the exact process through which a bill must pass before it becomes a law. Nor does it mention the congressional committees which have become so important and necessary to the passage of legislation. The parts of the lawmaking procedure and the machinery which were not provided for by the fundamental law have been supplied by Congress because they are necessary to the performance of its authorized functions.

This chapter outlines the organization of the legislative branch of our government, Congress, and it describes the matters listed in the Constitution concerning which the Congress may and may not pass laws. It also explains how Federal laws are passed by the Congress under a lawmaking system basically authorized by the Constitution and perfected throughout the years by the Congress itself.

NEW WORDS YOU WILL MEET

adjourn: end a meeting; continue until a later time

agriculture: relating to farming and farmers

appropriation: money set aside to pay for the cost of government and its related activities

assigned: appointed; given for a purpose; allotted

confirm: officially approve; ratify

convicts: finds or proves guilty of a crime

defeated: destroyed; beaten; disapproved

district: the part of a state which a Congressman (Representative) represents; geographical area set aside for a special purpose

general terms: not detailed; broad provisions and meanings

impeachment: accusation of serious misconduct by a government official in the performance of his public duties

implied: not written or stated, but understood to exist or follow as a natural result of something already written or stated

introduce: start; bring in

maintain: keep up; support; pay the cost of

militia: army of citizens trained for war or any other emergency; military force made up of citizens

participate: to take part in; have a share in

preside: to be in charge of a meeting; conduct a meeting

procedures: ways of doing things; methods by which things are done

referred: sent; turned over to

report: an account of something done, seen, heard, read, or considered; to furnish such an account

similar: alike in many, but not all, ways; basically or mostly the same

sources: places from which anything comes; beginnings of; origins of

standing committee: a permanent committee

vested: given to; placed with; conferred upon; belongs to

ORGANIZATION OF THE CONGRESS

The first sentence of Article I of the Constitution says:

All legislative powers herein granted shall be vested in a Con-

gress of the United States, which shall consist of a Senate and House of Representatives.

By these words the first authority or power that "We the People" delegated in the Constitution, the legislative or lawmaking power, was given to Congress.

Representation in the Senate

A Senator represents the people of the whole state.
The people of the whole state elect two Senators.
There are 100 members in the Senate.

Qualifications of a Senator

A Senator must be at least 30 years of age.
He must have been a citizen of the United States for at least 9 years.
He must be a resident of the state from which he is elected.

Term of Office of a Senator

Six years.
One-third of the Senators are elected every 2 years; in this way two-thirds of the Senators are always experienced legislators. They may be reelected.

Representation in the House of Representatives

A Representative acts for the people of the congressional district of the state in which he is elected.

Representatives are elected according to the number of people residing in a state. However small the population may be, its people are guaranteed at least one Representative. There are 435 members in the House of Representatives.

Qualifications of a Representative

A Representative must be at least 25 years of age.
He must have been a citizen of the United States for at least 7 years.
He must be a resident of the state from which he is elected.

Term of Office of a Representative

Two years.
The term of office of all Representatives ends on the same day; if they wish to return to Congress, they must be reelected.

Both Houses of Congress have equal authority in some matters. Each House has some power not given to the other. In this chapter you will learn how their powers are similar and different.

WHEN THE CONGRESS MEETS

Since every 2 years one-third of the Senators and all of the Representatives are elected, the life of a Congress lasts for 2 years. The 20th amendment provides that the Congress shall meet at noon on January 3 of each year, unless by law it provides for a different day. This meeting of Congress is called a regular session, and it continues until the members of both Houses decide to adjourn. A special session is one called by the President to consider problems which are so important that they require immediate attention and cannot wait until the next regular session.

SENATE AND HOUSE OFFICERS

The writers of the Constitution knew that the Senate and the House of Representatives would need officers to preside over their meetings and keep things running smoothly. They provided for certain officers and authorized each House of Congress to choose other needed officers.

Officers in the Senate

The Vice President of the United States is the President of the Senate and presides over its sessions.

The President of the Senate has no vote except in the case of a tie.

A President pro tempore presides if the Vice President is absent.

Additional officers are chosen by the Senators to perform other duties.

Officers in the House of Representatives

The Speaker of the House is chosen by its members and presides over its sessions.

By tradition the Speaker is a member of the political party to which most of the House members belong. As a result, he often has a great deal of influence in selecting members of important committees and in conducting the business of the House.

Additional officers are chosen by members of the House to perform other duties.

The members of each political party in each House of Congress select a "floor leader." He works to help pass laws which his party favors, and to defeat those laws which his party opposes. He is assisted by other Senators or Representatives who are members of his own party.

SENATE AND HOUSE COMMITTEES

A great deal of the work of both Houses of Congress is done by those legislators who are members of individual committees.

The Senate has 16 standing committees:

Aeronautical and Space Science
Agriculture and Forestry
Appropriations
Armed Services
Banking and Currency
Commerce
District of Columbia
Finance
Foreign Relations
Government Operations
Interior and Insular Affairs
Judiciary
Labor and Public Welfare
Post Office and Civil Service
Public Works
Rules and Administration

The House of Representatives has 20 standing committees:

Agriculture
Appropriations
Armed Services
Banking and Currency
District of Columbia
Education and Labor
Foreign Affairs
Government Operations
House Administration
Interior and Insular Affairs
Interstate and Foreign Commerce

Judiciary
Merchant Marine and Fisheries
Post Office and Civil Service
Public Works
Rules
Science and Astronautics
Un-American Activities
Veterans' Affairs
Ways and Means

From this study it can be seen that the Congress consists of a body of qualified Senators and Representatives, leaders who preside over the sessions of each legislative House, and committees of legislators whose main work is that of preparing bills for final action by the whole Congress.

AUTHORITY OF CONGRESS TO LEGISLATE

The Constitution gives to the Congress certain specific powers and authorizes it to pass all laws which may be necessary to put these powers into use and make them effective in carrying on the business of the government for the people. By reason of these specific powers and this broad legislative authority, the Congress has other powers not specifically listed in the Constitution. Although not written into the Constitution, these other powers are implied because, without them, the Congress could not make full use of the specific powers.

Some powers delegated to the Congress by the Constitution may be grouped under various headings:

Money and Trade

Under this heading Congress has the power to:

Provide for the coining of money and the regulation of its value
Borrow money
Levy and collect taxes
    The broad authority to pass all laws necessary to make effective the specific powers to borrow money, and to levy and collect taxes, also gives Congress an implied power to organize a system of banks.
Regulate commerce among the states and with foreign countries
    The writers of the Constitution probably realized that, with the natural growth of the nation, new kinds of commerce

would appear and should be regulated by Congress. Consequently, this power is expressed in general terms. The meaning of commerce is neither explained nor limited. As a result, it has been possible to hold that the telephone, telegraph, radio, and television systems are engaged in commerce and that the Congress has the power to pass laws regulating their operation in the interest of all the people of the United States.

National Defense

We the People of the United States, in order to . . . provide for the common defense . . . do ordain and establish this Constitution for the United States of America.

To achieve this objective of the Preamble, certain specific and implied powers are delegated to the Congress. Under the heading of National Defense, Congress has the power to:

Provide for the common defense
Provide and maintain an Army, a Navy, and an Air Force
    When the Constitution was written, the Founding Fathers could not have foreseen the possibility of an Air Force. However, the implied power of Congress to establish this branch of the Armed Forces under the broad national defense authority cannot be questioned.
Provide money for the Armed Forces, and regulate their size
Make rules governing the Armed Forces
Declare war
Aid in organizing and arming state militias (State National Guard units)
Call out the state militias in any national emergency

Other Authority

Other specific and implied powers delegated to the Congress fall within no one group. Under the heading of Other Authority, Congress has the power to:

Establish requirements and procedures for the naturalization of aliens
Establish a system of post offices
Establish a system of weights and measures
Pass laws governing the place in which the seat of the United States Government (District of Columbia) is located

The Similar Authority of Each House

Most powers delegated by the Constitution are vested in both Houses equally. Both can introduce bills to use the delegated powers listed above, except those which relate to the raising of money. However, each House has the authority to consider and vote for or against bills which carry out such powers, including those which are concerned with the raising of money.

Different Authority of Each House

Money bills cannot be introduced in the Senate. This very important power is given to the House of Representatives alone. Such bills must be proposed and passed first by the House of Representatives.

The Constitution also gives to each House additional powers not given to the other. The power of impeachment is given to the House of Representatives alone. Only the Senate, however, can try the official to determine whether he is guilty as accused. If the impeached official is found guilty by two-thirds of the Senate, he will be removed from public office and, perhaps, brought to trial before a regular court in criminal proceedings.

The Senate alone has the power to confirm the President's selection of persons to serve as members of his Cabinet, or to fill other important positions in the government.

Another power not shared with the House of Representatives is the Senate's authority to ratify a treaty between the United States and a foreign nation. Unless a treaty is ratified, it does not become effective.

Authority Denied to Both Houses

When the Constitution was written, the abuses which had caused the colonies to break away from Great Britain and declare their independence were fresh in the memories of its writers. They recalled all too clearly that the British King and Parliament had exercised lawmaking powers without the consent of the colonists. They were fearful that certain legislative powers given Congress might be used in a way that would be unfair and not in the best interests of the nation as a whole. To prevent this from happening, the Founding Fathers provided in the Constitution that Congress *shall not* have the power to:

Tax exports (goods shipped from one state to another or to a foreign country)

Pass trade laws favoring one state over another

Spend tax money unless a law has been passed authorizing it to be spent

> The law must show how the money will be spent and, from time to time, Congress must issue a report telling how public money has been spent.

Pass a law to punish a person for an offense that was not a crime when it was committed

Pass a law to deprive a person in jail of the right to be taken before a judge for the purpose of determining whether there is sufficient basis under the law to keep him in jail

> If the judge decides that there is no basis for holding the person in jail, he must be released.

Pass a law which convicts a person of an offense and sets forth his punishment

> In effect, this provision guarantees the right of an accused person to have a hearing in court before a judge and, if he wishes it, a trial by jury.

HOW A LAW BEGINS

A law begins as a proposal—a proposal to satisfy some public need or to solve a problem of the people through action by the lawmaking branch of the government. A proposal is called a bill when, in proper form, it is submitted by a legislator to Congress for consideration and action.

HOW A BILL IS PROPOSED

A bill can be submitted to the Congress only by a Senator or a Representative. However, a proposal of legislative action may come from any one of a number of different sources.

> People or organizations may suggest to a Senator or Representative that there is need for a new law, or a Senator or Representative himself may decide that a new law is needed.
>
> A standing committee of either House may prepare a bill to solve a problem relating to the work of that committee.
>
> A special committee appointed to study a particular problem may suggest that a bill be passed.
>
> The President may recommend legislation.

COMMITTEES STUDY ALL BILLS

Before a Senator or Representative can vote intelligently for or against any bill, it is necessary that he understand its provisions, why the law is needed, and the effect that it will have upon the people it is expected to benefit. This requires a careful study of the bill.

Thousands of bills are introduced in each House every year. Since it is not possible for every Senator and Representative to study all of these bills, much of the work is done by the standing committees and their subcommittees. Each House has its own committees.

Every bill introduced in Congress is assigned for study to a committee of the House in which it was introduced. The name of a committee describes the subject matter of the bills which are referred to it. For example, a bill introduced in the Senate and relating to labor matters would be assigned to the Labor and Public Welfare Committee of the Senate, as would a bill concerning social security.

Each standing committee has a chairman. More often than not, the committee chairman is a Senator or Representative who has served in Congress for many years. Usually he has had a great deal of experience with matters handled by the committee which he heads.

When the committee has finished its study of a bill, the bill is returned to the House from which it came, with a report of committee action. In this way, every member of each House has the benefit of the study made by its committees before he decides how to vote on a bill.

Examine the chart on the following page. It shows the steps that a bill must pass through from the time it is introduced until it is signed by the President and becomes a law.

Many bills never become laws. Some may be pigeon-holed and never acted upon by the committee. However, in the House of Representatives a majority of its members may sign a petition which will force the committee to return the bill to the whole House for debate and vote; in the Senate such a bill can be taken out of the committee when a majority of the Senators vote for such action. Other bills may be defeated by a final vote in either House of Congress. Still others may be defeated by a Presidential veto.

The President may veto a proposed law by refusing to sign it. When he vetoes a bill, the President returns it to the House which introduced it and tells why he opposes it. The bill can then be passed over the President's veto by a two-thirds vote of both Houses of Congress.

The President has 10 days in which to sign a bill. If he does not sign or veto it within that time, the bill becomes a law without his signature. If Congress adjourns within the 10 days allowed for the President to sign the bill, it does not become a law (unless he signs it within the 10 days). This is called a "pocket veto."

HOW A BILL BECOMES A LAW

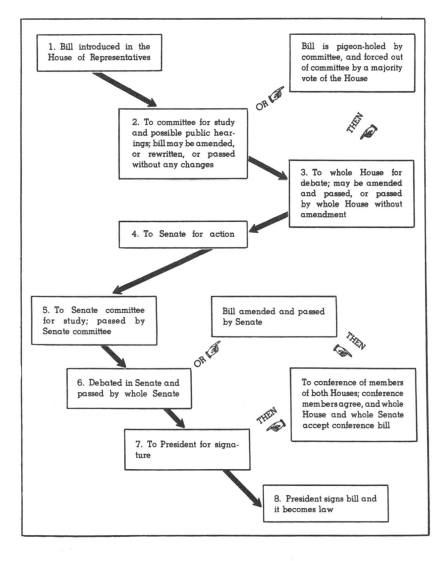

The people of the United States can participate in their government by recognizing the need for new laws and supporting Congress in its efforts to pass the necessary legislation.

NOW THINK ABOUT THIS

After each of the statements below the boxes, write in the House of Congress to which it relates:

The Senate	The House of Representatives

Member must have lived in the United States for 9 years _____.
Has at least one member from each state _____.
Member must be 25 years of age _____.
Members serve for 6 years _____.
Term of all members ends on the same day _____.
Each state elects two _____.
One-third of members are elected every 2 years _____.
Members serve for 2 years _____.

Answer briefly:
1. When does a regular session of Congress meet?
2. What determines the total number of Representatives from each state?
3. Who presides over the Senate?
4. Who presides over the House of Representatives?
5. What work is done by the standing committees of Congress?
6. How is it possible for Congress to pass laws relating to radio and television?
7. What is meant by "impeachment of a Federal officer"?
8. How is a bill proposed?
9. How is a bill vetoed?
10. How can a bill be defeated?
11. Where do all the money bills start?
12. What is the difference between a bill and a law?

Choose the word in the column on the left that has the same meaning as the underlined word(s) in the sentence:

militia   1. The Constitution gives Congress powers which are understood.

convicted   2. The man was proved guilty of the crime.

assigned   3. The governor called out the state's military force to
protect the people.

referred   4. The House sent the bill to the committee.

implied   5. The new Senator was appointed to the Foreign Relations Committee.

Talk about:

1. How does the organization of Congress carry out our principles of representative government?
2. Discuss the advantages of having all Representatives and only one-third of the Senators elected every 2 years.
3. Why does the Constitution list the kinds of authority Congress may not have?
4. Why is it important to have both Houses study a bill?

CHAPTER 7

The President—The Executive Branch of Our Government

Abraham Lincoln was one of the most beloved Presidents of the United States. He was President when the issues of slavery and secession were being decided. During this critical period, which saw the country involved in the Civil War, Lincoln led the fight to keep our nation together and to free the slaves.

Mr. Lincoln, our sixteenth President, was born in a tiny log cabin in Kentucky. His mother died when he was 9 years old. His step-mother encouraged "Abe," who was hungry for learning, to study and learn as much as he could. Although he attended school for a very short time, Lincoln educated himself by reading every book he could find or borrow.

When he was a young man, Lincoln found a set of old law books in a barrel. His reading of these books led to the beginning of a law career. His law career led to politics, and politics led to the Presidency.

Abraham Lincoln was one of our greatest Presidents. Many of his words are written in the hearts of all Americans.

He made one of the nation's most famous speeches at the dedication of our national cemetery at the site of the battle of Gettysburg (Pennsylvania). Imagine that you are listening to this tall, thin man as he sadly begins:

Fourscore and seven years ago our fathers brought forth on this continent a new nation, conceived in liberty, and dedicated to the proposition that all men are created equal. . . .

Look with him across the cold cemetery as he ends his speech with these stirring words:

. . . that we here highly resolve that these dead shall not have died in vain, that this nation, under God, shall have a new birth of freedom, and that government
> *of the people,*
>> *by the people,*
>>> *for the people,*
shall not perish from the earth.

In this chapter you will read about the duties and powers of the President of the United States.

NEW WORDS YOU WILL MEET

agencies: organized groups of officials or other persons selected to do some special job, or to administer a law or laws

campaign: organized action to produce a certain result, such as winning an election; to take such action

crisis: a time when difficult decisions must be made; turning point

depression: a period of unemployment and widespread poverty

entitled: given a claim or right to

injustice: violation of a right; inequity; a wrong; unfairness

negotiate: discuss and arrange terms; consult

nobility: people of high rank, title, or birth

pardons: official orders forgiving a crime

popularity: being liked by most people

prestige: reputation, influence, or distinction based on what is known of one's abilities, achievements, opportunities, associations, etc.

reprieves: temporary delays in carrying out punishment

secession: the right of a state to leave the Union

title: name showing rank, position, or condition in life

Fill in each blank in the sentences below with the proper word from the list above:

1. The Secretary of State helps to _____ treaties with other countries.

2. During the Civil War _____ of the states was an issue.

3. In a time of national _____ the President is often given more power.

4. After a candidate has been nominated, he begins his _____ for office.

THE PRESIDENT—THE EXECUTIVE BRANCH

In the 1600 block of Pennsylvania Avenue in Washington, the District of Columbia, there is only one house. It is the White House, the home of the President of the United States. In another country the home of the chief executive would be called a palace and the master of the house would have a title of nobility. Article I, Section 9, of the Constitution states that no person shall be granted a title of nobility by the United States. Therefore, it is "Mr. President," one of the citizens, who lives in the White House.

Article II of the Constitution gives the President the executive power to carry out the laws of the nation. It states that the President shall be a natural-born citizen, at least 35 years of age, and a resident of the United States for at least 14 years. The Constitution also provides for the payment of a salary to him, and describes his duties and powers. It further declares that the President shall be elected by electors chosen in a manner provided by the state legislatures and shall serve for a term of 4 years. Amendment 22 states that no President shall be elected more than twice.

The Constitution also describes how the President may be removed from office and provides that upon his removal, or upon his death, his duties shall be carried out by the Vice President. The Presidential Succession Act of 1947 provides that, in case of the death or removal from office of the President and Vice President, they shall be succeeded by (1) the Speaker of the House, (2) the President pro tempore of the Senate, and (3) the Cabinet members in the order, generally, in which their offices were created.

HOW A PRESIDENT IS NOMINATED

The nominating procedure is just as important in a democracy as the election procedure. The nomination of candidates answers the question, "Who will run for office?"

No single nominating procedure is used in the United States. Since 1840, however, the convention system has been used to nominate candidates for President and Vice President. During the summer of the year in which a President is to be elected, each political party holds a national convention. The members of the party in each state send delegates to the convention. They elect officers for the convention and agree on a party platform. The delegates are then ready to select the party's candidate for President.

There is first a roll call of the states. As the name of each state is called, a delegate from that state may offer the name of a person to represent the party as its candidate for President.

When the delegates of every state have had an opportunity to name their candidates, the roll of states is called again, and all of the delegates vote to determine which one of the proposed candidates will receive the nomination. The candidate who receives a majority of the votes is nominated for the office of President.

The candidate for Vice President is chosen in the same way that the candidate for President is selected.

Candidates conduct their campaigns for the offices of President and Vice President until the election, which is held on the first Tuesday after the first Monday in November.

HOW A PRESIDENT IS ELECTED

The chief executive is chosen officially by the presidential electors from all the states. Every state is entitled to have as many electors as it has Senators and Representatives in Congress. When the citizens of a state vote for President, they actually vote for a group of electors who have promised to choose as President a particular candidate. The voters have the opportunity to vote for any one of the candidates because in every state there will be a group of electors for each candidate. The group of electors receiving the most votes becomes the electors for the state. After the citizens have voted, each group of electors chosen meets in its own state and votes for the President in accordance with the group's promise. By this indirect method, the voting citizens actually elect the President.

When Congress meets in January after the election, the members of the two Houses officially count the votes of the electors. The candidate who receives a majority of the total number of electoral votes is elected President. If no candidate receives a majority of the electoral votes, the House of Representatives chooses the President from among the three candidates who received the highest number of votes.

The Vice President is elected in the same way, and for the same 4-year term of office. Should no candidate for Vice President receive a majority of the electoral votes, the Senate chooses as Vice President one of the two candidates who received the highest number of votes.

Because the votes of the citizens actually elect the President, the people know who has been elected as soon as the votes for the electors have been counted. This is usually the day after the election.

THE PRESIDENTIAL INAUGURATION

The day the President begins his term of office is known as Inauguration Day. On this day, the 20th of January following his election, the President takes the oath of office. It is administered to him by the Chief Justice of the United States.

The President repeats the oath which is required by the Constitution—the same oath taken by George Washington on April 30, 1789.

Following the oath, the new President makes a speech, called his inaugural address. In this speech he tells what he expects to do and what he would like to have done within the next four years. Many people hear this speech on the radio. Others watch the President take the oath and listen to his speech on television. Some read the inaugural address in the newspapers. A great many people go to Washington to see and hear this impressive ceremony.

THE POWERS OF THE PRESIDENT

The President of the United States has the most important elective office in the world today. The Constitution gives him the executive power of the nation. He also has certain legislative and judicial powers.

As chief executive of the nation, the President's first duty is to see that Federal laws and treaties are properly enforced. In doing so, he issues necessary orders and instructions.

The Constitution provides that he shall be the commander in chief of the Army and the Navy, and of the militia of the various states when they are called into Federal service. He may send our Armed Forces to any part of the world.

THE PRESIDENT'S AUTHORITY
TO APPOINT FEDERAL OFFICERS

The President has authority under the Constitution to appoint certain officers of the United States, but the Constitution states that the Senate must approve these appointments. Using this authority, the President appoints the heads of the 12 executive departments and some of their branches, members of independent executive agencies, and other Federal officials. There are many of these officers in the government. Before making appointments to Federal jobs in a particular state, the President often consults the Senators from that state,

especially if they are of his political party. This is called "Senatorial Courtesy."

THE PRESIDENT'S AUTHORITY
TO WORK WITH FOREIGN COUNTRIES

The President directs foreign relations through his power to nominate the Secretary of State, and the ambassadors, ministers, and consular officials who represent the United States abroad.

Government officers of foreign nations consider the President and his Secretary of State to be the representatives of the United States who are responsible for making and maintaining friendly relations with their countries. The President and his Secretary of State have the power to carry on all official contact with foreign nations, to arrange through the Department of State for the protection of our citizens who travel abroad, and to protect foreign persons traveling in the United States. The President receives representatives of foreign countries. He has the authority to recognize, or refuse to recognize, a new nation or a new government.

He has the power to negotiate and enter into treaties with other nations, with the approval of the Senate. He may make executive agreements, which do not need Senate approval, with foreign countries.

THE LAWMAKING AUTHORITY
OF THE PRESIDENT

The Constitution gives the President some control in lawmaking. You will remember that bills passed by Congress are sent to the President and that he may sign or veto them. Sometimes he will tell his party members in Congress that he intends to veto a certain bill and, as a result, Congress may not pass the bill. The President may even use his personal influence and prestige with members of Congress to obtain legislation.

Each year, as required by the Constitution, the President reports to the Congress on the state of the Union. In his State of the Union Message, he talks about the needs of the people, about our relations with other countries, and usually recommends legislation which he believes to be necessary for the nation. He may also send a special message to Congress for similar purposes. If necessary, he may call Congress into a special session, as provided by the Constitution, and recommend legislation to solve a particular problem. When Congress

does not respond to his wishes, he may call upon the people directly for support. He does this through the press, radio, and television.

THE JUDICIAL AUTHORITY OF THE PRESIDENT

The President has the authority to select and appoint judges of the Supreme Court, and other Federal courts, provided the Senate approves his nominations.

Many of the 55 men who helped to frame the Constitution were very able lawyers. They had learned that sometimes even a judge may not be fair, or he may make an honest mistake. These wise leaders believed that injustice would not happen often, but they wanted someone to help the person wrongly convicted. Therefore, authority was given to the President to grant reprieves and pardons to persons convicted in Federal courts. He cannot, however, pardon lawbreakers who have been sentenced by a state court, nor can he pardon any government official for a Federal offense which resulted in his impeachment and conviction.

As you can see, the President has many powers. How he uses his powers determines whether he is a weak or strong leader. His personal popularity with the people can help him win support for his programs. If he is serving during a time of national crisis, as in wartime or in a depression, he is usually given more power.

Although the President of the United States has great power because he is the executive authority of the nation, he remains "Mr. President," resident of the White House, whose work is to lead the nation and serve the will of the people.

NOW THINK ABOUT THIS

Explain the meaning of the underlined part of each of the following sentences:

1. The chief executive is chosen officially by presidential electors.
2. The President reports on the state of the Union in his annual message to Congress.
3. The President of the United States has the most important elective office in the world today.
4. The Constitution says that no person shall be given a title of nobility.
5. The President's personal popularity with the people helps win support for his programs.

6. Even a judge may make an honest mistake.
7. Election day is the first Tuesday after the first Monday in November.

Answer "yes" or "no" to each of the following questions, and tell the reason(s) for your answer:
1. Is it the first duty of the President to make the laws of the nation?
2. Does the Vice President become President if the President dies?
3. Are the President and the Vice President elected by a direct vote of the people?
4. Is the President elected to serve for a certain number of years?
5. Can a naturalized citizen of the United States become President?
6. Does the President have authority to call special sessions of Congress?
7. Does "Senatorial Courtesy" mean the respect that the Senators pay to the President?

Talk about:
1. How are candidates for President nominated?
2. What is meant when it is said that a President may be a "strong" or "weak" leader?

CHAPTER 8

The Cabinet
Advises the President

The newspapers are filled with examples of democracy in action. Read these familiar everyday headlines:

Senate Discusses New Treaty
NATO Chiefs Meet in Brussels
Government Hopes to Avoid Railroad Strike
New Regulations for Zoning Mail Announced
Record Farm Production in '66
New Income Tax Law Passed by House

If we read the stories under the headlines, we will notice that they concern problems relating to foreign affairs, national defense, labor unions, the post office, farm production, and income for the Federal Government. We will also notice a common thread that runs through all the articles: the important role played by the President in helping to solve these problems. Actually, they are only a few of the many problems which are considered by our President, and this should make us realize how great his fund of knowledge must be if he is to handle them and all the other problems which he must help to solve. We should also realize the great amount of work which must be done to solve the problems described in the newspaper stories. No single individual, not even the President, could possibly know about and handle all of these matters without assistance. For this reason, the President has a Cabinet. Each member of the Cabinet is a skilled administrator and heads one of the large executive departments. The members of the Cabinet are well informed concerning the matters handled by the departments they head, and they act as advisers to the President and assist him in solving problems relating to such matters.
This chapter tells about the work of the President's Cabinet.

NEW WORDS YOU WILL MEET

civil service: having to do with working for the government of a nation or state

classifies: groups according to some system; divides into groups

conservation: preserving from harm or decay; protecting from loss or from being used up

counterfeit: imitation; false; to make false money

duplication: the doing again of something that has already been done

estimates: judgments or opinions about how much, how many, how good; evaluations

handicapped: disabled; not able to do something because of a disadvantage or disability

initiate: begin; set things going; introduce

national security: the safety of the nation

natural resources: things that come from nature

objectionable: unacceptable; likely to be opposed; offensive

patent: a government grant to a person stating that he is the only one allowed to make or sell a new invention for a certain number of years.

policy: plan for present or future official action

prosecute: to take action to convict a person of a crime

research: careful hunting for facts or truth

urban: relating to cities and towns

vocational training: education to prepare a person for some new job or kind of work

ADVISING THE PRESIDENT—THE CABINET

The first Congress of the United States met in 1789. One of its first acts was to provide for a group of men to advise and assist President Washington. This group of advisers soon came to be known as the President's Cabinet. It consisted of a Secretary of State, a Secretary of the Treasury, and a Secretary of War, each of whom headed an executive department, and an Attorney General and a Postmaster General.

The President's Cabinet today has 12 members. The titles of these Cabinet members and the year in which their departments were officially created by Act of Congress are:

Secretary of State (1789)

Secretary of the Treasury (1789)

Secretary of Defense (First called Secretary of War (1789); Department of Defense (1949) includes former Departments of War (1789), Navy (1798), Air Force (1947))

Attorney General (The office of Attorney General (1789) heads the Department of Justice (1870))

Postmaster General (The office of Postmaster General (1789) heads the Post Office Department (1872))

Secretary of the Interior (1849)

Secretary of Agriculture (1862) (Commissoner of Agriculture renamed Secretary of Agriculture (1889))

Secretary of Commerce (1913) (First called Secretary of Commerce and Labor (1903))

Secretary of Labor (1913)

Secretary of Health, Education, and Welfare (1953)

Secretary of Housing and Urban Development (1965)

Secretary of Transportation (1966)

HOW CABINET MEMBERS ARE CHOSEN

Soon after he has been inaugurated, the President chooses his Cabinet. In appointing Cabinet members, the President is guided by a number of considerations. First, he chooses people who are experienced in the affairs of the departments which they are to head. Second, he selects men whose ideas of government are like his own, men who believe in the policies and program of his party. Third, he usually selects people from his own political party, although he is not required to do so. Finally, he tries to put together a Cabinet whose members come from different parts of the country. This is done in order to give all sections of the country representation in the executive branch of the Federal Government. Appointments to the Cabinet, like appointments to all important Federal offices, must be approved by the Senate.

HOW THE CABINET OFFICER
DOES HIS WORK

Cabinet members always keep in touch with the President. They do this by private conference, telephone, or messenger. As a general rule, the entire Cabinet meets with the President once a week. In all of his contacts with the President, the Cabinet member suggests and advises. Guided by this advice, the President makes the final decision on all important matters of policy. He is basically responsible for the operation of the various executive departments of the government.

Each Cabinet member also administers the work of the executive department which he heads. He, too, has many assistants, some of whom are appointed by the President, and many others who are selected only after having passed a civil service examination to qualify for appointment. Some officers and employees work in branch offices of the executive departments which are located in many parts of the country.

DUTIES OF THE CABINET

The Department of State

The Secretary of State ranks as the executive officer next in importance to the President and the Vice President. The President relies on the Secretary and his department to initiate and develop the country's foreign policy and to recommend action to put it into effect. The Secretary and his assistants also represent the President in dealings with officials of countries all over the world.

The Department of State works in many ways to establish and maintain friendly and peaceful relations between the United States and foreign countries. The department acts, through United States representatives to the United Nations, with other countries to settle differences which might lead to war. It also assists the President in negotiating and carrying out treaties with foreign countries. Educational information activities abroad, and foreign student and teacher exchange programs, are also planned and supervised by this department to further the general objectives.

State Department representatives who are assigned abroad meet with citizens of foreign countries who wish to come to the United States, and issue permits (visas) allowing them to apply for admission to this country.

This department issues United States passports to citizens who desire to travel abroad for pleasure or business. It also helps our businessmen by reporting on trade conditions and acting in a general way as agent for United States business interests abroad.

The Department of the Treasury

The Secretary of the Treasury is the President's adviser on the financial affairs of our country. He is in charge of collecting and managing the funds of the United States.

The Department of the Treasury handles more money than any other organization in the world. It is responsible for the coining and printing of the nation's money, bonds, and stamps; the borrowing of money as directed by Congress; and the payment of all debts of the nation. The collection of Federal taxes, including taxes on many kinds of goods brought into the country, is a further responsibility of the Treasury Department.

The Secret Service, under direction of the Secretary of the Treasury, is responsible for the guarding of the President and his family, as well as other high government officials. However, another very important duty of this agency is the investigation and arrest of persons who are believed to have made or passed counterfeit money.

Other units of the Treasury Department guard the seacoasts and the land borders of the United States to protect shipping and prevent the bringing of goods into the country without the payment of taxes; still other units administer laws relating to alcohol and narcotics.

The Department of Defense

The Secretary of Defense, as a member of the President's Cabinet, is adviser to the President on all military matters. He is responsible for our national defense and national security. He establishes general policies for, and supervises, all branches of the Armed Forces, as well as certain nonmilitary activities; prevents duplication and overlapping in the purchase of military supplies, and directs the preparation of the budget estimates for the Armed Forces.

The Department of Defense is subdivided into three military departments, the Department of the Army, the Department of the Navy, and the Department of the Air Force. Each of these departments is headed by a secretary who does not, however, have the rank of a Cabinet member. Each military department has many responsibilities relating to its branch of the Armed Forces and, as required by its own functions,

Recruits and trains officers and enlisted personnel, and makes provision for obtaining military equipment and weapons for their use,

Acquires and maintains forts, camps, naval bases, and air bases, as appropriate to their particular operation,

Conducts research on new weapons, and

Participates in space programs which relate to military matters.

The Department of Justice

The Attorney General advises the President in all legal matters pertaining to the Federal Government.

The Department of Justice assists the President by providing the means to enforce Federal laws. The Attorney General is the chief legal officer of the nation and he, or his assistants, represent the United States in all proceedings before the Supreme Court. The President is assisted by this department in protecting rights guaranteed by the Consitution.

Under the supervision of the Department of Justice is the Federal Bureau of Investigation, which conducts investigations to determine whether Federal laws have been violated. The department takes action to prosecute and convict persons who are accused of Federal violations. It maintains and supervises Federal institutions in which lawbreakers are imprisoned as punishment for their crimes.

Another important function of the Justice Department is the administration and enforcement of the immigration and naturalization laws.

The Post Office Department

The Postmaster General advises the President on matters concerning the mail. He supervises the work of the department, its many offices and divisions. With the approval of the President, he also makes postal agreements with foreign governments.

The Post Office Department establishes and maintains post offices, classifies and delivers mail, keeps objectionable materials from the mails, and posts announcements of civil service examinations.

The Department of the Interior

The Secretary of the Interior advises the President on matters relating to the development and conservation of our natural resources, and matters relating to island possessions of the United States.

The Department of the Interior administers and enforces the Federal laws relating to the public lands of the United States including, among others, our national parks and lands reserved for fish and wildlife conservation. It supervises the operation of power plants which provide electricity for large parts of the country; helps to develop operating procedures and safety programs for removal from the earth of its natural resources, such as coal, gas, and oil.

The Department of the Interior administers many Federal laws relating to the island possessions of the United States. It is responsible also for the welfare of American Indians living on reservations in the United States.

The Department of Agriculture

The Secretary of Agriculture keeps the President advised concerning problems of the American farmer. One of the ways he carries on research, education, and conservation projects relating to agriculture is by working in close cooperation with state research stations.

The Department of Agriculture helps farmers learn the best ways to develop better crops and livestock by teaching them the science of soil care, and helping them to fight plant and animal diseases. It gives them information about the supply and prices of farm products and helps them obtain a fair price for their products. This department assists in financing the construction of rural electric systems, and provides a credit system for farmers.

The Department of Commerce

The Secretary of Commerce advises the President concerning the nation's business affairs. He promotes and develops the foreign and domestic commerce of the United States.

The Department of Commerce collects information and publishes reports on goods produced, exported, imported, and stocked in the United States; establishes and maintains official standards of weights and measures; and issues patents and administers patent laws. This department also issues official weather reports and forecasts; studies the seacoasts and rivers and reports on tides and currents to safeguard shipping; studies transportation and travel, both in the United States and abroad; and takes the census of the nation every 10 years.

The Department of Labor

The Secretary of Labor advises the President on the welfare of the wage earners in the United States. He tries to improve working conditions as directed by laws of Congress.

The Department of Labor administers and enforces the labor laws including those relating to the wages, hours of work, working conditions and welfare of young people who work and women who work. It helps to set up and enforce safety programs, and tries to prevent or settle strikes. It administers the programs of unemployment insurance and workmen's compensation. This department collects information and publishes reports about employment, wages, and the welfare of workers.

The Department of Health, Education, and Welfare

The Secretary of Health, Education, and Welfare advises the President on matters regarding the general welfare of the people. He acts to improve the mental and physical health of the people through research and the efficient and proper use of new knowledge.

The Department of Health, Education, and Welfare works through a Public Health Service to prevent and control disease, and through the Food and Drug Administration to assure the purity and quality of the foods, drugs, and cosmetics we use. The department provides vocational training for physically handicapped persons, including war-disabled civilians. It administers the social security programs and certifies Treasury Department grants to states for maternal and child health services. The Department of Health, Education, and Welfare helps to improve education in our country.

The Department of Housing and Urban Development

The Secretary of Housing and Urban Development advises the President with respect to Federal programs and activities relating to housing and urban development.

The Department of Housing and Urban Development is concerned with housing, urban development and urban transportation, including the encouragement of private homebuilding and mortgage lending, and the furnishing of information to aid state, county, and other local governments in solving community and metropolitan development problems.

The Department of Transportation

The Secretary of Transportation, the newest member of the President's Cabinet, is the President's principal adviser on all transportation matters.

The Department of Transportation conducts research in the field of transporation to find safer, faster, and cheaper ways of moving people and freight throughout the United States. In order to establish transportation policies which will serve the needs of the public, as well as of private industry, labor, and the national defense, the department seeks the cooperation of Federal, state, and local governments on transportation problems.

The work of the executive departments, under the administration of members of the President's Cabinet, affects every individual in this country. If a person is serving in the Armed Forces, his activities are regulated by the Department of Defense. If he is a farmer, he has direct contact with the Department of Agriculture. If he has an income, he may pay income taxes to the Internal Revenue Service of the Department of the Treasury. Should he be an alien, he will be in touch with the Immigration and Naturalization Service, of the Department of Justice, from the time of his application for admission to the United States until he is granted citizenship.

In addition to the 12 executive departments, there are many independent agencies in the Federal Government, each one having certain duties and responsibilities, as indicated often by their names. They are, to name a few, the Atomic Energy Commission, Farm Credit Administration, Federal Communications Commission, Labor Relations Board, Small Business Administration, and Civil Service Commission. The head of each independent agency is directly responsible to the President.

Good citizens will always use their right to vote and will elect a President who they believe will appoint the most capable men to Cabinet positions and to head the independent agencies.

NOW THINK ABOUT THIS

Select the word under each sentence that best completes the sentence:
1. The committee chairman will _____ a discussion of the bill.
     initiate   research   classify
2. The Department of Commerce issues _____ and administers laws relating to them.
     reports   visas   patents
3. Doctors depend upon _____ in order to win their fight against disease.
     lawyers   research   books
4. If you do that work, it will be a _____ of what was done earlier.
     duplication   service   policy
5. Many people find the use of that word _____.
     supervised   objectionable   conservation

Answer the following questions:
1. The head of which department advises the President about legal matters?

2. What is the work of the Post Office Department?
3. In which department is the Weather Bureau?
4. How does the Department of Health, Education, and Welfare help the people?
5. Which department helps farmers develop better crops and livestock?
6. How many Cabinet members are there?
7. How are the Cabinet members chosen?
8. Which department coins money?
9. Which department works with the United Nations?
10. Which department maintains our national parks?

Talk about:
1. For what reasons was the President's Cabinet enlarged?
2. How does each Federal department affect the daily life of the people?

CHAPTER 9

The Courts—The Judicial Branch of Our Government

You must recall certain things if you are to understand one of the most important duties of the judicial branch of the government. The Federal Constitution gave specific powers to Congress and, in addition, gave it authority to pass all laws which might be necessary to use those powers. This last authority is so broad and general that it is possible for Congress to make a mistake and use that authority to pass a law which it has no power to pass. Furthermore, laws passed by Congress are not always clear and, in enforcing them, the executive branch of the government may give them meaning not intended by Congress. Such laws and their enforcement might take away rights or freedoms of the people.

The government created by the Constitution protects these rights and freedoms through a system of Federal courts. The Constitution provides that:

The judicial power of the United States shall be vested in one Supreme Court, and in such inferior courts as the Congress may from time to time ordain and establish.

The Supreme Court of the United States meets in the Supreme Court Building in Washington, D.C. It is a beautiful building of white marble. The figures over the entrance represent our national ideas of law and liberty. Above the main entrance appear the words, "Equal Justice Under Law."

The Supreme Court, made up of a Chief Justice and eight Associate Justices, is usually in session from October to June. One of the most important duties of the justices is to decide whether laws passed by the Congress agree with the Constitution. The justices do this by interpreting and explaining the laws of Congress and the provisions of the Constitution. Should the Supreme Court decide that the Constitution does not give Congress the power to pass a certain law, the court declares that law to be unconstitutional. Such a law can no longer be enforced by the President and his executive officers.

John Marshall, a brilliant lawyer who also fought under Washington during the War for Independence, was Chief Justice of the Supreme Court when it was first decided in 1803 that the Supreme Court had the authority to declare that a law passed by Congress did not agree with the Constitution. Nonetheless, Chief Justice Marshall himself believed that the Founding Fathers intended the Federal Government to be a strong government, and that it should have enough power to govern the nation for the benefit of the people. He interpreted the Constitution in a way that gave the government this needed strength without destroying the rights and freedoms of the people. It has been said that he gave life and power to the Constitution.

William Howard Taft, another great Chief Justice of the Supreme Court, said that the reason for the existence of the courts is to promote the happiness of all the people by the speedy and careful administration of justice. He believed that the courts were created to help individuals who seek justice.

As you study this chapter, you will learn how the judicial branch of our government serves the people and protects their freedom.

NEW WORDS YOU WILL MEET

appeal: to request a higher court to review a lower court's decision; also, the request itself

award: money or some other thing of value given in payment of a claim decided in one's favor

customs: taxes or money charged on something imported or brought into the country from another country; import taxes

diplomatic: having to do with the official activities of government officials who work with representatives of other countries

dispute: quarrel; argument; difference of opinion

jurisdiction: authority of the government or an agency of the government to exercise control over people or property; authority of a court to hear and decide a criminal or civil case

resign: to give up a position or job

self-restraint: a restriction by a person of his own actions; self-control

INTERPRETING THE LAWS— THE JUDICIAL BRANCH

The Supreme Court alone is named and created by Article III of the Constitution. However, the Constitution also gives Congress the authority to establish other courts, and to increase or decrease their number, as the need may arise. From time to time Congress has used that authority to create the lower Federal courts which exist today.

By creating the Supreme Court and authorizing the establishment of other Federal courts, the Constitution created the judicial power; that is, the power to hear and decide the two classes of cases— criminal and civil.

Certain things which a person may do will harm other persons. To protect all the people from the effect of these acts, the Congress passed laws making them crimes. The laws provide for the punishment of persons who commit these acts. If a person breaks one of these laws, the Federal Government will prosecute him in court. This is called a criminal case. Persons convicted in a criminal case may be punished by imprisonment. You will remember that the 6th amendment of the Constitution guarantees a trial by jury to every person accused of a crime.

It is also possible for a person to take some action that affects the rights of another person. Such action, however, may not be a crime because no criminal law has been broken. In such a case one person can sue the other person in court. This is called a civil case. A person who is found to be wrong in a civil case is never punished by being sent to prison, as in a criminal case, but the court may make him pay a certain sum of money to the other person. Such money payment is called damages.

THE JUDGES OF THE FEDERAL COURTS

An independent judiciary, free from control by the King, was proposed in England during the 17th century. The authors of the Constitution adopted this idea when they included in the fundamental law provisions regulating the appointment of judges to the Supreme Court and the lower Federal courts.

The Founding Fathers provided that the President shall appoint all Federal judges, with the consent of the Senate, and that a Federal judge shall hold office during "good behavior." He can be removed from office only by Congress upon impeachment for, and conviction of, "high crimes and misdemeanors." Otherwise, every judge is appointed for life, or until he chooses to resign. The Constitution provides further that the salary of a Federal judge shall not be reduced while he is in office. The judges, therefore, are independent and cannot be influenced by other branches of the government, or by any person or group of persons.

THE AUTHORITY OF THE FEDERAL COURTS

Article III of the Constitution gives to the Federal courts jurisdiction in a case because of its subject matter. Upon this basis, the jurisdiction of the courts may include cases which concern the interpretation of the Constitution, of treaties between the United States and foreign countries, of laws which relate to shipping on the high seas, and of all other Federal laws. All cases involving a violation of Federal criminal laws are heard in a Federal court. They include cases relating to internal security, immigration, and customs matters. In addition, the Federal courts have authority to handle cases involving laws relating to interstate commerce.

Federal courts also are given jurisdiction in a case because it involves certain parties. A case involving the United States as a party must be heard in a Federal court. Also heard in a Federal court may be a case involving two or more states, or two citizens of different states. Suits between a foreign government or one of its citizens and one of our states may be heard in a Federal court.

THE SUPREME COURT

The Chief Justice and the eight Associate Justices of the Supreme Court sit as a group. When the court hears a case, it is decided by a majority vote of the justices.

The Supreme Court is primarily an appellate court; that is, a court which hears appeals from decisions made in cases which began in a lower court. The Constitution, however, provides that in all cases affecting foreign diplomatic officials, such as ambassadors and other public ministers and consuls, the Supreme Court shall have original jurisdiction. This means that such cases can be heard only in the Supreme Court. Because the authority in these cases comes from the Constitution, Congress cannot take it away from the court.

The Supreme Court has the power to declare that a law passed by Congress and approved by the President is unconstitutional. It also has the authority to decide whether a state constitution or a state law agrees or disagrees with the Federal Constitution. The decision of this, the highest Federal court, is final. With a final decision, there can be no further appeals.

The Supreme Court has developed a tradition of self-restraint, and is generally very careful in declaring state or Federal actions unconstitutional. It does not consider all new laws, but only those that may be involved in a case that is brought before the court for decision.

CHECKING THE POWER OF THE SUPREME COURT

The Constitution grants Congress and the President some control over the Supreme Court.

The President appoints all Federal judges, with the consent of the Senate. He also has the power to grant pardons and reprieves to persons who have been convicted of crimes in Federal courts.

The Congress determines the number of justices of the Supreme Court, and it fixes their pay. The Senate has authority to approve or disapprove appointments of men selected by the President to be justices of the Court. Except as otherwise provided in the Constitution, the Congress as a whole has the authority to decide what cases will begin in the Supreme Court, rather than in a lower Federal court, and what cases started in the lower Federal courts may be appealed to the Supreme Court. However, the Court is allowed to decide which of the appealed cases it will consider.

OTHER FEDERAL COURTS

Not long after the inauguration of George Washington as our first President, Congress used the authority given to it in the Constitution and passed the Judiciary Act of September 24, 1789. This act established a system of lower Federal courts, which consisted of 13 district courts and three circuit courts. As the country grew and the need for more courts arose, additional courts were created by Congress. Today each state has at least one district court, and the larger states have two or more such courts.

The United States courts of appeals were established in 1891 to relieve the Supreme Court of many of the cases that were being appealed to it from the district courts. At the present time, the country is divided into 11 judicial circuits, each having a circuit court of appeals. Each court of appeals has from three to nine judges. One justice of the Supreme Court is also assigned as a circuit justice for each circuit.

The lowest Federal courts are the United States district courts.

They have original jurisdiction in all cases that may be heard by the Federal courts, except those which come within the original jurisdiction of the Supreme Court, or the jurisdiction of special courts. District court cases are usually heard by a single judge and sometimes with a jury. Usually an appeal from the decision of a district court may be taken to a United States court of appeals for the judicial circuit within which the district court is located. In some cases, a further appeal may be taken to the Supreme Court.

Congress also recognized the need for special courts. It set up the United States Court of Claims in 1855, a kind of court called the Board of United States General Appraisers in 1890, and the United States Court of Customs and Patent Appeals in 1909. In 1926 the name of the Board of United States General Appraisers was changed to the United States Customs Court. The United States Court of Military Appeals was established in 1950.

During the early days of our country, a person who had a reasonable money claim against the Government of the United States had to ask Congress to pay the claim. The United States Court of Claims was established to relieve Congress of the burden of deciding whether such a claim should be paid. This court consists of a Chief Judge and four Associate Judges who meet in Washington. The awards of this court cannot be paid until Congress appropriates the money to pay them.

The United States Customs Court hears and settles disputes that arise out of decisions by customs officers relating to customs matters. For example, decisions as to the rate of tax on, or the value for tax purposes of, the article imported may be reviewed by this court. Appeals from these decisions are heard by the United States Court of Customs and Patent Appeals, as are appeals from decisions relating to patent matters. An inventor, for example, who has been denied a patent by the Patent Office may bring his appeal in this court.

Members of the Armed Forces who are accused of misconduct may be tried by court-martial (a military court). Decisions in the more serious cases can be appealed to the United States Court of Military Appeals.

Final appeal of decisions in cases arising in the special courts may be taken to the Supreme Court, except decisions of the Court of Military Appeals. Decisions of this court are final.

THE FEDERAL COURTS AND THE PEOPLE

The chief purpose of the Federal courts, and all courts, is to help the people settle their disputes and differences fairly and peaceably.

The courts provide justice for all. The people may not always like the laws, but it is their duty to obey them as they are explained by the courts. When the people do not like the laws, they can elect representatives who will change them. Any change in a law must be made in the manner provided for by our plan of government.

It is the duty of the courts to make sure that all laws agree with the Constitution of the United States.

The judicial branch is the balance wheel in our system of government. It helps to maintain the correct constitutional relationships between the executive and legislative branches of the Federal government, and also between the nation and the states.

NOW THINK ABOUT THIS

The following sentences are separated into two parts. Match the first part of each sentence in Column A with its other part in Column B:

Column A	Column B
1. Article III of the Constitution describes the	a. relating to shipping on the high seas.
2. Violations of Federal law	b. that a law passed by Congress is unconstitutional.
3. Federal courts have jurisdiction over cases	c. were originally handled by Congress.
4. Claims against the government of the United States	d. are handled by the Federal courts.
5. The Supreme Court can declare	e. is never sent to prison.
6. A person found wrong in a civil case	f. Federal courts and their authority.

Answer the following questions.
1. Which court is the only one named in the Constitution?
2. What is an appellate court?
3. Who hears cases in a United States district court?
4. Who has the power to establish lower Federal courts?
5. How many Federal judicial circuits are there in the United States?
6. What did John Marshall do to strengthen the Federal government?
7. How could the executive branch, in enforcing a law, give it a meaning not intended by Congress?

8. Why are the judges of Federal courts independent and free from influence by others?

Talk about:
1. What are the special courts and their duties?
2. Why is a system of courts necessary in a democracy?

CHAPTER 10

Each State
Has a Government

You will recall that 13 colonies had governments based upon colonial charters, rather than constitutions. By 1775, however, these established governments were gradually falling apart because of the troubles with England. The Second Continental Congress then urged each colony to adopt such form of government as would guarantee the highest degree of happiness and safety for its people. In January of 1776 New Hampshire became the first of the 13 colonies to form an independent government under a constitution. Thereafter, South Carolina took similar action, as did most of the other colonies or states. The colonial charters of Connecticut and Rhode Island served as their constitutions for a number of years after they became states. Massachusetts approved a state constitution in 1780 which, although somewhat revised, continues to be the basis for that state's government.

While there were differences in each of the new state constitutions, certain things were similar. Each one recognized that the government could exercise only those powers granted to it by the people, and that the people had rights which the government must respect. The constitutions also divided the government into three branches—the executive, the legislative, and the judicial—with each branch having some controls over the others. It can be seen, therefore, that people in the United States actually live under Federal and state governments which are very similar in form.

The United States Constitution gives to the states those powers which are not granted to the Federal Government and, at the same time, not denied to the states by the Constitution. Throughout our history this division of power has caused conflicts between Federal and state governments over the authority of each. For example, Congress passed the Tariff Act of 1828 which placed high taxes on imported goods. This pleased the northern states because it protected the sale of their manufactured products. The southern states, however, disliked the tax because it affected the exchange of their cotton, tobacco, and other products for goods manufactured in foreign countries. This tax brought about one of the first conflicts involving the authority of the Federal and state governments.

The southern states argued that the Federal Government had been created by the states and, therefore, each state had the right to determine whether a law passed by the Congress was authorized by the Constitution. They further claimed that, if a particular state decided the Constitution did not give Congress the power to pass a certain law, the state did not have to obey it. This idea became the basis for what is known as the doctrine of "states' rights."

A famous debate on states' rights took place in the Senate in 1830. Senator Robert Hayne of South Carolina argued that his state had the right to decide that the Constitution did not give Congress the authority to pass the Tariff Act. Speaking for the northern states, Daniel Webster, a Senator from Massachusetts, answered by saying that the Federal Government was created by the people and not by the states, and that the United States would soon break apart if each state insisted on obeying only those laws which it chose to accept. He ended his speech by saying, ". . . Liberty and Union, now and forever, one and inseparable!"

Webster was defending Article VI of the Constitution which declares that the Constitution shall be the supreme law of the land and shall determine what powers are given to the Federal and the state governments. He stressed the fact that under the Constitution the powers to govern are shared by the national and state governments. He argued that when the Federal Government acts in accordance with the powers granted to it by the Constitution no state can nullify that action.

In this chapter you will read about the organization of the state governments.

NEW WORDS YOU WILL MEET

auditor: a person whose duty it is to examine financial records

convenience: comfort; advantage; benefit

doctrine: a belief in certain things; a set of principles accepted as true

exchange: the trading of one thing for another; to give one thing in trade for another

inseparable: cannot be divided; must remain together

nullify: to wipe out or destroy; to make meaningless

utility: a service or product that is useful

ORGANIZATION OF OUR STATE GOVERNMENTS

The first 13 states had constitutions when the Constitution of the United States was written. The state constitutions gave to their people certain rights and a representative form of government which were very important to them.

Many people believed that the new Federal Government might take away some of these rights or might change the form of the state governments. With this in mind, the writers of the Constitution made provision for the states to keep many of their rights, and further guaranteed to each state a republican, or representative, form of government. However, because the Federal Constitution also provides that it shall be the supreme law of the land, every state is bound by it and all state constitutions and laws must agree with it.

CONTENT OF STATE CONSTITUTIONS

The constitution of each state provides the general plan for that state's government. It may also set forth the basis for other governments within the state, such as those of counties and towns. Other state constitutions may also establish governments for their larger cities.

A state constitution usually describes the purposes for which the state government is being created and lists the rights of the people living in that state. All of the constitutions declare that the final authority to govern belongs to the people of the state. They also tell how the government of the state and its communities shall be organized. Each state constitution generally lists the authority of each branch of the state government, establishes rules for the local governments, and provides a method for amending the constitution. It may also list different kinds of property that shall not be taxed by the state government.

GOVERNMENT ORGANIZATIONS ARE SIMILAR

The Federal and state, as well as the city, governments in the United States each have three branches of government. The following chart shows how the organization of government in the nation, the states, and the cities is similar.

	FEDERAL	STATE	CITY
Legislative Branch	Congress—Senate and House of Representatives	State legislature— two houses in all states except Nebraska	City council or commission
Executive Branch	President, Vice President, and President's Cabinet	Governor and governor's assistants	Mayor or city manager or city commission, and assistants
Judicial Branch	Supreme Court Federal courts	State courts	City courts

THE LAWMAKING BRANCH OF STATE GOVERNMENTS

In all of the states except Nebraska, which has one lawmaking body, the legislative branch of the state governments has two houses. This is similar to the Federal Government. The upper house is called the senate. The lower house may be called the house of representatives or the assembly. These legislatures may vary in size. In most states there are more members in the house of representatives than in the senate. Both senators and representatives must be chosen on the basis of population. The term of office of state legislators is whatever the state law declares it to be, usually two years.

State legislatures make laws in the same general way as the Congress of the United States. All members in each house cannot study every bill. Therefore, each house has a committee system similar to that of Congress. Each bill is referred to the committee organized to handle the subject matter to which the bill relates.

Any member in either house can introduce a bill.

The bill is then referred to the appropriate committee of that house for study.

If the committee approves the bill, it will be returned for consideration by the house from which it came.

After members speak for or against the bill, a vote is taken.

If the bill receives a majority of votes, it will be passed by that house.

If a bill has been passed in one house, it will be sent to the other house where it will go through the same procedure as it did in the first house.

If the bill is passed in both houses, it will be sent to the governor of the state.

If the governor signs the bill, it will become a law; if he vetoes it, the bill can become a law only if it is again voted upon by both houses and passed by the necessary number of votes.

THE EXECUTIVE BRANCH OF STATE GOVERNMENTS

The chief executive in every state is the *governor*. His qualifications and term of office are determined by the state constitution. The governor has executive officers to help him carry out his responsibilities. These officers may be appointed by the governor or may be elected by the people.

The governor, together with his executive officers, enforces the laws of the state and sees to it that the work of the various departments is done properly. He may also suggest to the legislature what laws should be passed or changed. In some states the governor may appoint judges to state courts, while in other states judges may be elected by the people.

A majority of the states has:

A *secretary of state* who keeps the official records of the state.

An *attorney general* who is the chief law officer in the state. He advises the governor in legal matters, and helps to convict and to punish people who break the state laws. He represents the state in the courts.

A *state treasurer* who takes care of the state's money that comes from taxes, licenses, and fees. He also pays the debts of the state.

A *state auditor* who examines all the financial records of the state and the books of public officers.

The states generally have special officers whose duty it is to enforce labor laws. Other special officers enforce laws relating to the operation of public utility companies which furnish the people of a community with gas, water, and electricity. Each state also has special groups, called *boards* or *commissions,* that administer other state laws.

THE JUDICIAL BRANCH
OF STATE GOVERNMENTS

Every state government has a judicial branch consisting of a large number of lower state courts which have authority to try the two classes of cases—criminal and civil. Almost all civil and criminal cases involving state laws are first tried in these lower courts.

All states have higher courts which study the decisions appealed from the lower courts. These courts of appeals decide whether or not the correct decisions were made in the lower courts. The appeals court may agree with the decision of the lower court and dismiss the appeal. On the other hand, if it is found that a case was not correctly decided, the case can be sent back to the lower court for further hearing, or the court of appeals can change the decision of the lower court.

States can create courts to hear special matters. For example, there may be a children's court to try cases of children accused of having broken the law, and a court of domestic relations to hear cases involving disagreements between husband and wife.

Every state has a state court which is similar in function to the United States Supreme Court. Such a court has power to review decisions of the lower state courts, and its decisions interpreting the constitution and laws of the state are final.

THE STATE HELPS TO GUARD
THE HEALTH OF ITS PEOPLE

One of the most important services of a state is the protection of the health of its people. Most states have laws requiring that doctors, nurses, and persons who sell drugs have licenses. These people must pass state examinations before licenses will be issued to them. The state examines many foods and drugs to be certain that they are pure. It establishes and maintains state hospitals for its people, and provides health examinations for schoolchildren.

THE STATE EDUCATES ITS PEOPLE

State governments do many things to help educate their people. Each state sets certain standards of education for its schools. It passes laws that require children to attend school—public elementary schools and high schools are free. The state usually provides money to a school according to its needs. Many states establish and maintain colleges and universities where some, or all, of the expenses are paid from taxes. Most states provide adult education classes.

THE STATE PROTECTS THE LIVES
AND PROPERTY OF ITS PEOPLE

The authority of a state to protect the lives and property of its people is called its "police power." This police power provides for the safety, comfort, and convenience of the people. Every state has a state police force. It also has a militia that can be called upon to work with local and state officers to protect the people and their property.

The state protects its people by regulating certain kinds of industry. Special officers inspect restaurants, factories, mines, and other places where people work. This is done to make certain that these places are clean and safe. By such inspection the hours during which women and children work are also kept within legal limits. Public utility companies are regulated and the people are benefited by the establishment of fair rates for utilities, and are assured that health and safety standards are maintained.

THE STATE CARES
FOR ITS OWN PROBLEMS

When a country is new and it has many natural resources, such as rich soil, forests, oil, gas, and coal, people may become careless. They may forget to think about the millions of people who will live in the country years later. Should the people become careless, the soil may become poor, the forests may be cut down, and the oil, gas, and coal may be used up. The country would then be poor.

For many years the Federal Government and the states have been teaching the citizens to care for natural resources. They try to teach the people how to keep soil from washing away, to plant crops so that one crop puts back into the soil what another crop used up in growing, to plant new trees as older trees are cut, and to preserve oil and natural gas supplies. By saving natural resources, our country will remain rich for posterity.

Most roads are under the control of local governments, but, since they are used by all the people of the state, part of the cost of building and repairing many local roads is paid by the state. The state and Federal governments work together in planning, building, and paying for cross-country highways.

Every day, in many ways, the state is part of the life of the people. They must help the state and themselves by obeying the laws, paying their taxes, working for better laws, and supporting law officers in carrying out their duties.

Each state is as good as the people who live in it. The state can be no better than its people.

NOW THINK ABOUT THIS

Complete each of the sentences below with the correct word(s) from this group:

commission   posterity   stressed
license   products   domestic relations

1. A person must pass a state examination before he can get a _____ to sell drugs.
2. The _____ court tried to bring the husband and wife together.
3. A special group called a _____ administers some state laws.
4. The governor _____ the need for new legislation.
5. Conservation assures to _____ the benefit of our natural resources.

Answer these questions:

1. How did the writers of the Constitution make provision for the states to keep many of their rights?
2. Name the two houses of the legislative branch of state governments.
3. Which state has only one legislative house?
4. How can a bill become a law if the governor vetoes it?
5. Who is the executive authority of the state?
6. Which officers help the governor and how are they chosen?
7. What are some of the special courts which the state can create?
8. Over what cases do the state courts have authority?
9. What provisions do state constitutions contain?
10. What are some very important services which the state provides?

Talk about:

1. How are the three branches of the Federal and the state governments similar?
2. How does a state take care of its own problems?
3. Why can we say that a state is no better than the people who live in it?

CHAPTER 11

Our Local Governments

Two of the most important issues of our time are world peace and the preservation of democracy. In both of these related issues the Federal Government plays a key role. It is natural, therefore, for Americans to follow with great interest the activities of the three branches of our Federal Government. This is as it should be, since democracy depends on a body of informed citizens.

The activities of the governments closer to us also deserve our attention. The work of our state government affects our daily lives in many ways. There are few citizens who do not vote, travel on highways, or pay taxes. All of these things are regulated, in one way or another, by the state government.

An informed citizen should also be interested in his local government. It is at this level that most people are in the closest contact with their elected and appointed officials. The laws made and enforced by these officials affect everyday services of importance to us like trash removal, parking, water supply, and street lighting. This is why a good citizen must be well informed about local affairs, as well as state and Federal affairs.

The purpose of this chapter is to describe local government in the United States. As you read, learn how local government varies in different parts of our country and then find out how the government in your local community compares with the governments described in the chapter.

NEW WORDS YOU WILL MEET

assessor: person who fixes the value of something, usually for tax purposes

boundaries: things that indicate limits; dividing lines

council: a group of men elected to help govern a local community

deeds: legal documents that transfer ownership of real estate

disposal: the getting rid of something; the removal of

engineer: to plan or build; a person who plans or builds
facilities: things used or needed to do something easily
mortgage: a legal paper transferring property as security for a loan
with the understanding that the property will be returned when the
loan is paid; written pledge of property to secure a loan
recreation: refreshing activity; enjoyable relaxation; play, not work
reject: refuse to accept
summons: notice to a person to appear in court

ORGANIZATION OF OUR LOCAL GOVERNMENTS

The people who first came to America believed in the right of self-
government. These early settlers made and enforced the laws of the
communities in which they lived.

The general purpose of local government is to provide the people
with safe and better living conditions. To accomplish this purpose a
local government must provide many services. Among the things that
are needed for safe and better living are good schools; pure water
supply; health regulations controlling the disposal of sewage, garbage,
and trash; good street lighting; parks and other facilities for recreation; and police and fire protection.

Local governments levy community taxes to pay for these things.
Some local services, like education, are usually paid for by both the
state and local governments.

The area of each state is divided into various parts, and each of
these parts has some form of local government. These parts may be
called counties, cities, towns (townships), or villages, and each one
of them may be a unit of local government. Usually a larger unit of
local government includes one or more of the smaller units. Some large
cities are both a city and a county.

All local communities and their governments are organized under
authority of the state government or state constitutions. Many local
governments are granted charters by the state providing for a plan
of government.

COUNTY GOVERNMENTS

The county is the most important local government in a majority of
the states. A *board of commissioners,* or a *board of supervisors,* is usually in charge of this unit of government. The members of the board
are elected by the people of the county, as are most of the other county
government officials.

Officials in county government may differ from one county to another. Certain officers, however, are generally common to most counties in our states. These are:

The *county clerk* who serves as a secretary for the county board. He issues marriage licenses and birth certificates. In some states the county clerk is in charge of preparing ballots for voting, and recording results of elections.

The *county treasurer* who controls the finances of the county. He pays bills when such payments are authorized by the commissioners or supervisors.

The *recorder of deeds* who keeps a record of deeds and mortgages. In some states the work of the recorder of deeds is done by the county clerk.

The *county auditor* who examines the financial records of the county officers.

The *county engineer* who plans and directs the building of roads and other county construction.

The *sheriff* whose duty it is to preserve the peace, serve summonses, and supervise the jail of the county.

The *county attorney* who prosecutes criminal cases which arise within the county.

A *superintendent of schools* who handles matters relating to education in the county.

CITY GOVERNMENTS

Elected representatives direct the government of the city. They make the local laws for the comfort, convenience, safety, and protection of the people and set the tax rate to raise the money to pay for these services.

Each city has a head of the government, usually called the *mayor* or the *city manager*. However, in some cities a *commission* may head the government. City governments also have various executive departments. They usually include a department of public health, as well as police, fire, and sanitation departments.

City governments also have a school system which, in many cities, is headed by a *board of education* whose members are elected by the people. A *superintendent of schools* is usually appointed by the board members to supervise the schools in the city.

City government usually has one of the following plans:

The Mayor-Council Plan

The mayor-council plan is the oldest form of city government in the United States. Under this plan the voters elect a mayor and a lawmaking group called a *council*. A member of the council may be elected by all of the voters in a city, or only by those voters in his section of the city. In the mayor-council plan of city government, the council makes the laws and the mayor enforces them.

Like the President of the United States or the governor of a state, the mayor administers the different executive departments of the city government. The head of each of these departments is usually appointed by the mayor, and has such authority as may be delegated to him by the mayor or by the city council.

The laws passed by the council are the laws of the city. City laws are called ordinances. Each ordinance must be in agreement with the city charter which, in turn, must also agree with all the state and Federal laws. With the help of the mayor, the city council decides how much money is needed by each department of the city government. Taxes are then levied to raise the needed funds.

The City Manager Plan

Under the city manager plan of local government the people elect a council. The council, which is the legislative body of the city, hires a city manager, a person who is trained in directing the work of local governments. It is the responsibility of the city manager to enforce the laws of the city. He has authority to appoint the heads of the various executive departments of the city government. They assist the city manager in the enforcement of the city's laws. He, aided by the department heads, may suggest ways to improve the services of the city, or to cut down the cost of government. The council can accept or reject these suggestions. Whenever the council so desires, it may remove the city manager from office.

The Commission Plan

Under the commission plan of city government, the voters elect a small group of officials, called a commission. The members of the commission are called *commissioners*. The voters of the whole city usually elect all of the commissioners. However, some cities may be divided into sections and the voters of each section may elect one commissioner.

Each member of the commission helps to make and administer the laws of the city, and he usually heads one or more of the executive departments of the city's government.

TOWN OR VILLAGE GOVERNMENTS

In the New England states—Connecticut, Maine, Massachusetts, New Hampshire, Rhode Island, and Vermont—the town is an important unit of local government. In this area of the country many people live in towns, in villages, and on farms. The town government usually has jurisdiction over an area of from 25 to 40 square miles. People living on farms may come under the town or village government.

The basis of town government is the town meeting which is generally held once a year. All qualified voters in the town may go to this meeting for the purpose of fixing the tax rate, making appropriations, and selecting officials for the town government. Sometimes, in the larger towns, not all of the voters attend the town meeting. Instead, they select a certain number of the voters to represent them at the meeting. This is called a representative town meeting.

The town or village may have all, or only some, of the following officers:

> Members of a *board* or *council* who both make and enforce the laws. (In New England, board members are called selectmen.)
>
> A *clerk* who keeps records of board meetings or council meetings, and who registers and files legal papers such as birth and death certificates, deeds, and mortgages.
>
> A *tax assessor* who fixes the value of property on which taxes are to be paid.
>
> Members of a *school board* who are responsible for the schools.
>
> A *treasurer* who collects money and pays bills at the request of the board or council.
>
> A *constable, firemen,* and *health officers* who protect lives, health, and property.

TOWNSHIP GOVERNMENTS

The township may be the local unit of government within the county. In areas of the country where it does exist, the township government is somewhat similar to the town government of the New England states.

DIFFERENT GOVERNMENTS WORK TOGETHER

Counties, cities, towns, or whatever a local unit of government may be called, help the state government, as well as the local community.

Within their boundaries, they help to enforce the state laws, collect state taxes, assist in state elections, and cooperate with the state in many other ways.

They owe their existence to the state under whose authority they were created. The state determines the limits beyond which local governments may not go but, otherwise, it generally does not interfere in local affairs.

ALL COMMUNITIES HAVE A SYSTEM OF COURTS

Every unit of local government has, to some extent, a system of courts. The judges of these courts may be elected by the people, appointed by the city council or commissioner, the governor of the state, or some other authorized person or group of persons.

Local self-government in this country is as old as the first settlement. As we fight to defend our nation, we fight to defend our right to local self-government.

NOW THINK ABOUT THIS

Use each of the following phrases in a sentence of your own:
1. right of self-government
2. reject a suggestion
3. accomplish this purpose
4. owe their existence
5. hires a city manager
6. section of a city

Answer the following questions:
1. What is the purpose of local government?
2. What does the county auditor do?
3. How are judges of local courts selected?
4. In the mayor-council plan of government, what does the council do?
5. In the commission plan of government, what does each commissioner do?
6. For what purpose is a town meeting held?

Talk about:
1. Why is the mayor or a city manager one of the most important persons in city government?
2. What is meant when we say that local communities cooperate with the state?

CHAPTER 12

The Importance
of Your Vote

The truths set forth in the Declaration of Independence may be described as the foundation of the American way of life. To insure the rights of life, liberty, and the pursuit of happiness, the writers of the Constitution formed a democracy, a government deriving its "just powers from the consent of the governed."

The people of the United States are "the governed." They are governed by their own consent which is given when they vote. In a democracy the people first decide, and then make known by their votes, who will govern them and how they will be governed. You will read in this chapter about the political party system and the importance of voting.

NEW WORDS YOU WILL MEET

acquainted: informed about; have knowledge of
candidate: a person seeking office; a person who runs for office
consent: approval; agreement
considered: thought about; gave attention to; studied, or examined
deriving: getting; receiving; obtaining
extension: expansion; continuation; addition
frequently: often; many times
insure: make safe; guarantee; protect
majority: more than one-half
nominate: to name or choose a person to be considered for office
urge: plead with; earnestly request
various: different; several or many; a number of

VOTING—A RIGHT AND A DUTY

You have learned that the people of the United States have the final authority to govern. By voting, they delegate that authority to others who will then represent them in carrying on the work of the government.

WHO CAN VOTE

After the Civil War the right to vote was given to former slaves. Under the 15th amendment to the Constitution, no citizen can be refused the right to vote because of his race, color, or because he has been a slave. The 19th amendment gave women the right to vote.

Not every citizen is eligible to vote, however, because each state can, and has, set up additional qualifications for voters. For example, until the 24th amendment was adopted, citizens living in a few states could not vote there for President, Vice President, or members of the Congress unless they had paid a poll tax. Common to all states are their laws requiring that a voter be a United States citizen, and a resident for a certain length of time in the place within the state where his vote will be cast. Each state sets an age limit for voting. The voting age is 18 years in two states, 19 years in a third, and 20 years in a fourth state. The age limit in all other states is 21 years. In some states a citizen must be able to read and write before he can vote. States try to give the right to vote only to those citizens who understand what it means to vote.

You will always want to use your right to vote. You should find out what you must do to qualify under the law of the state in which you make your home. Most states also require a citizen to register before election day with election officials in the place where he lives. At that time, he must establish his qualifications to vote and have his name placed on a voting list. As soon as you become a citizen you should register to vote in the community where you make your home. Then, when election time comes, vote—and never fail to vote. It is your duty as a citizen to vote. In this way you use your authority to govern.

HOW THE FINAL AUTHORITY TO GOVERNMENT IS USED

By his vote a citizen influences the government in many ways. His vote helps to elect officers who make and enforce the laws of the nation, the state, and the city or town in which he lives.

As a qualified voter, you can vote for or against proposed amendments to the constitution of your state. Often you will be asked to vote on special issues concerning the spending of money for highways, schools, water systems, or other public projects. State constitutions and city charters frequently declare that the right to borrow money above a certain amount must be decided by the voters. Sometimes a state legislature will be unwilling to take final action to pass an especially important law until the citizens first express their approval by voting for it.

When a citizen votes he indicates his own personal choice. However, the will of the majority of voters is expressed in the final results of most elections. A majority means more than one-half of the votes cast. Many elections and public issues in the United States are decided by a majority vote.

In an election three or more candidates will often seek the same public office, and no one candidate may receive a majority of all votes cast. Sometimes, such an election will be decided by a plurality; that is, the winning candidate will be the one who receives the highest number of votes, even though he gets less than a majority. The difference between the number of votes cast for the winning candidate and the number given to the candidate receiving the next highest number of votes is called a plurality.

A citizen has a duty to vote, as well as a right to vote. He should give serious thought before making his choice of candidates. A good citizen votes in every election. Only in this way can we have a government by the people.

FORMING OPINIONS

The decisions which a voter is required to make on important issues are a serious responsibility. Such decisions may affect our lives, liberty, and property. But, meeting the responsibility of making decisions helps free people keep their freedoms. Every citizen has a duty to keep himself informed about candidates and issues. Before he forms opinions and makes decisions, he should read, listen, and think—then he can vote for what he believes is right.

SHARING OPINIONS

Although a citizen can and should vote as he wishes, he ought to be interested in what other people are thinking and saying. By obtaining the opinions of others concerning issues in government, the citizen can learn all sides of a question and this will help him make a good decision when he casts his vote. Citizens can learn about the opinions of others in many ways. Public issues and government matters can be discussed at home, in a person's neighborhood, and at work. Much can be learned about how others think by watching television, listening to the radio, and reading newspapers and other printed materials.

An intelligent voter reads more than one paper, magazine, or book, in order to get different opinions about candidates, party platforms, and issues.

A citizen of this country should want to know what other voters think about questions of the day, but the final decision as to how he will vote should be his own. However, his decision should be made only after he has heard all sides of the various questions.

THE POLITICAL PARTY SYSTEM

A citizen can also learn how others think by becoming acquainted with the political party system. A political party is a group of people who work together as an organization to get the kind of government action they believe in and want.

Political parties have helped to make our plan of government work. They are an extension of the democratic ideas first developed by the Constitution. Although the Constitution makes provisions for the election and appointment of persons to offices in government, it says nothing about how persons shall be nominated, or chosen to be considered, for these positions. Nominees are usually chosen by political parties in accordance with methods and practices that have been developed over the years. The methods by which candidates are nominated are just as much a part of our plan of government as if they had been written into the Constitution. They are a part of the American tradition which has added to the growth of the Constitution without its amendment. Without them, provisions of the Constitution could not be put into effect.

PARTY PLATFORM

Members and leaders of each party prepare a statement setting forth the aims and objectives of the party. This statement is called the party platform. The platform makes known the position of the party and its members on important public questions and affairs of government. It may call for more, fewer, or different taxes. It may recommend changes in the powers delegated by the people to their elected representatives.

NOMINATION OF CANDIDATES

Most men and women who seek election to public offices are nominated by a political party. Once they are nominated, they are called candidates for election.

Candidates of a political party may be nominated at a primary election. This is a special election at which the registered voters of each party are given an opportunity to choose candidates who will represent their party in a general election. In a primary election, citizens can vote only for the nominees of the party with which they are registered.

Candidates can also be nominated by a convention. Members of a political party select and send delegates to a meeting place. After considering the qualifications of possible candidates, the delegates choose those who will represent the party. The candidates for President and Vice President are nominated in this manner at a national convention.

A number of states allow a person to be nominated by petition. This is done by having qualified voters sign a petition requesting that a certain citizen's name be placed on the ballot. Men and women nominated in this way are called independent candidates.

THE VOTER AND HIS PARTY

Each political party would like to have the voters elect its candidates to a majority of the public offices. Such a majority would give the party the power to carry out its aims and objectives as stated in the party platform.

Each political party tries to gain the support of as many voters as possible. One way used to gain public support is by holding meetings to which all voters are invited. Copies of the party platform are given to the voters at the meetings. Members and leaders of the party make speeches and urge the voters to elect its candidates. Booklets are also given out which show what the men in office have, or have not, done and what the candidates of the party promise to do if they are elected, or reelected. A citizen may join any party and may attend its meetings and serve on committees. He can make speeches and give copies of the party platform to other voters. He can ask voters to support the candidates of his party.

Joining a political party is one of the most effective ways for a citizen to take part in government. However, it is not the only way. A citizen is not required to become a member of a political party. In fact, many wish to be, and they are, listed as independent voters. A voter is free to change to another party if he wishes to do so. He does this at registration time.

ELECTION DAY

After a candidate has been nominated to run for public office, he must be elected by the people. This is done at a general election. A general election is one in which only one candidate from among those nominated is chosen by the voters to fill the office for which they all ran.

In a general election a person may vote for the candidates of any party.

THE SPIRIT OF DEMOCRACY
IN THE UNITED STATES

The people of the United States decide public questions by votes—not by force. The voters may make a mistake and elect a person who does not perform his duty properly. They can correct this error in judgment by replacing him with another person at the next election for the office to which he was elected.

NOW THINK ABOUT THIS

Explain the underlined part of each sentence:
1. What does consent of the governed mean?
2. What does support a candidate mean?
3. What does the extension of democratic ideas mean?
4. What does nominate a candidate mean?
5. What does sign a petition mean?

Answer the following questions:
1. Who is eligible to vote in the United States?
2. What are some of the issues that citizens are asked to vote on?
3. What is a majority vote?
4. What is meant by an independent candidate?
5. How can a citizen learn what other people think about candidates or issues?
6. What is meant by a party platform?

Talk about:
1. Why is voting a serious responsibility?
2. Why is it necessary to register?

CHAPTER 13

Our Flag

Every nation in the world has its own flag. A flag identifies a country and symbolizes the hope and pride the citizens feel for their nation.

The story of the flag of the United States of America, often known as "Old Glory," the "Stars and Stripes," or the "Red, White, and Blue," parallels the story of the United States itself. George Washington recognized this when he described our flag: "We take the stars from heaven, the red from our mother country, separating it by white stripes, thus showing that we have separated from her, and the white stripes shall go down to posterity representing liberty." Today we think of each color in the flag as symbolizing one of the American ideals: the red is for courage, the white for truth, and the blue for justice. We must think of and work for these ideals each time we see our flag flying over "the land of the free and the home of the brave."

NEW WORDS YOU WILL MEET

allegiance: devotion and loyalty to something or someone
motto: a word or sentence appropriate to something
posterity: the future; succeeding generations
symbolize: to represent or express something by the use of a mark or picture
union: the blue field and white stars at the upper left corner of the flag of the United States

ITS HISTORY AND REGULATIONS

EARLY AMERICAN FLAGS

Before the Revolutionary War, the flag generally flown by the American colonies was the flag of Great Britain.

Early in the revolutionary period the colonists asserted their dissatisfaction with Britain by adopting new flags. Each colony had its own flag, frequently the colonial coat of arms with some motto. The colonists also chose designs that symbolized their struggle with the wilderness of the new land. Beavers, anchors, and pine trees, or "liberty trees," were seen on many banners. The rattlesnake was a popular device. Flags appeared showing the rattlesnake with thirteen rattles, representing the thirteen colonies, and mottoes like "Don't Tread on Me" and "Unite or Die."

THE GRAND UNION FLAG

The first flag of the colonists to have any resemblance to the present Stars and Stripes was the Grand Union flag. It consisted of thirteen stripes, alternating red and white, standing for the thirteen colonies, and retained the Union Jack, the flag of Great Britain, in the upper left corner, indicating that the colonists still recognized their union with the mother country. In January 1776, the Grand Union flag became the standard of the Continental Army.

A NEW FLAG FOR A NEW COUNTRY

On June 14, 1777, the Continental Congress adopted a new flag. Like the Grand Union flag, this flag had a field of thirteen red and white stripes, but instead of the Union Jack it had a union of thirteen white stars on a blue ground. The colonists had declared freedom the previous year and the new flag was another way of asserting their freedom from England. According to tradition, Betsy Ross made this first flag. Today we celebrate the date of its adoption as Flag Day.

A STAR FOR EACH STATE

Our flag remained the same until 1795 when two new stars and two new stripes were added for the new states of Kentucky and Vermont.

In 1818, after the admission of five new states, Congress realized how confused and crowded the flag would become if a new stripe were to be added for each new state. It was therefore decided that the flag should always retain thirteen stripes, representing the original colonies, and that a star should be added to the blue field for every new state entering the Union.

Our flag now proudly displays fifty stars for each of the fifty states:

Alabama, Alaska, Arizona, Arkansas, California, Colorado, Connecticut, Delaware, Florida, Georgia, Hawaii, Idaho, Illinois, Indiana, Iowa, Kansas, Kentucky, Louisiana, Maine, Maryland, Massachusetts, Michigan, Minnesota, Mississippi, Missouri, Montana, Nebraska, Nevada, New Hampshire, New Jersey, New Mexico, New York, North Carolina, North Dakota, Ohio, Oklahoma, Oregon, Pennsylvania, Rhode Island, South Carolina, South Dakota, Tennessee, Texas, Utah, Vermont, Virginia, Washington, West Virginia, Wisconsin, Wyoming.

FLAG REGULATIONS

There are many rules and customs pertaining to the use and display of the flag of the United States of America. These are the most important:

The flag should be displayed every day from sunrise to sunset.

The flag should be displayed daily on or near every public building and every schoolhouse.

When carried in procession with other flags, the American flag should always have the place of honor.

Respect should always be shown to the flag.

The flag should never touch the ground or anything else beneath it.

The flag should never be used for advertising purposes.

When the flag becomes old and worn it should be burned in a respectful manner.

THE PLEDGE OF ALLEGIANCE TO THE FLAG

One of the ways we can show our respect and love for our flag is by saying the Pledge of Allegiance:

I pledge allegiance to the flag of the United States of America and to the Republic for which it stands, one Nation under God, indivisible, with liberty and justice for all.

NOW THINK ABOUT THIS

Select from the list below the word that best completes each sentence:

Old Glory

rattlesnake

burned

courage

advertising

1. The American flag is affectionately known as _____.
2. The red stripes in our flag symbolize the American ideal of _____.
3. The _____ was a popular device on many flags of the pre-Revolutionary period.
4. The flag should never be used for _____ purposes.
5. When the flag becomes too old for use it should be _____.

Answer briefly:

1. Before the Revolutionary War, why did the colonists use the flag of Great Britain?
2. What was the first colonial flag to resemble the present Stars and Stripes?
3. Why does the flag have thirteen stripes?
4. Who, according to tradition, made the first American flag?

Talk about:

1. What does the Pledge of Allegiance mean to you?
2. Why are there rules concerning the use and display of the American flag?

Appendix

THE DECLARATION OF INDEPENDENCE

IN CONGRESS, JULY 4, 1776

The Unanimous Declaration of the Thirteen United States of America

When in the course of human events, it becomes necessary for one people to dissolve the political bands which have connected them with another, and to assume among the powers of the earth, the separate and equal station to which the laws of Nature and of Nature's God entitle them, a decent respect to the opinions of mankind requires that they should declare the causes which impel them to the separation.

We hold these truths to be self-evident, that all men are created equal, that they are endowed by their Creator with certain unalienable rights, that among these are life, liberty and the pursuit of happiness. That to secure these rights, governments are instituted among men, deriving their just powers from the consent of the governed,—That whenever any form of government becomes destructive of these ends, it is the right of the people to alter or to abolish it, and to institute new government, laying its foundation on such principles and organizing its powers in such form, as to them shall seem most likely to effect their safety and happiness. Prudence, indeed, will dictate that governments long established should not be changed for light and transient causes; and accordingly all experience hath shown, that mankind are more disposed to suffer, while evils are sufferable, than to right themselves by abolishing the forms to which they are accustomed. But when a long train of abuses and usurpations, pursuing invariably the same object evinces a design to reduce them under absolute despotism, it is their right, it is their duty, to throw off such government, and to provide new guards for their future security.—Such has been the patient sufferance of these Colonies; and such is now the necessity which constrains them to alter their former systems of government. The history of the present King of Great Britain is a history of repeated injuries and usurpations, all having in direct object the establishment of an absolute tyranny over these States. To prove this, let facts be submitted to a candid world.

He has refused his assent to laws, the most wholesome and necessary for the public good.

He has forbidden his Governors to pass laws of immediate and pressing importance, unless suspended in their operation till his assent should be obtained; and when so suspended, he has utterly neglected to attend to them.

He has refused to pass other laws for the accommodation of large districts of people, unless those people would relinquish the right of representation in the legislature, a right inestimable to them and formidable to tyrants only.

He has called together legislative bodies at places unusual, uncomfortable, and distant from the depository of their public records, for the sole purpose of fatiguing them into compliance with his measures.

He has dissolved Representative Houses repeatedly, for opposing with manly firmness his invasions on the rights of the people.

He has refused for a long time, after such dissolutions, to cause others to be elected; whereby the legislative powers, incapable of annihilation, have returned to the people at large for their exercise; the State remaining in the mean time exposed to all the dangers of invasion from without, and convulsions within.

He has endeavoured to prevent the population of these States; for that purpose obstructing the laws for naturalization of foreigners; refusing to pass others to encourage their migrations hither, and raising the conditions of new appropriations of lands.

He has obstructed the administration of justice, by refusing his assent to laws for establishing judiciary powers.

He has made judges dependent on his will alone, for the tenure of their offices, and the amount and payment of their salaries.

He has erected a multitude of new offices, and sent hither swarms of officers to harass our people, and eat out their substance.

He has kept among us, in times of peace, standing armies without the consent of our legislatures.

He has affected to render the military independent of and superior to the civil power.

He has combined with others to subject us to a jurisdiction foreign to our constitution, and unacknowledged by our laws; giving his assent to their acts of pretended legislation:

For quartering large bodies of armed troops among us:

For protecting them, by a mock trial, from punishment for any murders which they should commit on the inhabitants of these States:

For cutting off our trade with all parts of the world:

For imposing taxes on us without our consent:

For depriving us in many cases, of the benefits of trial by jury:

For transporting us beyond seas to be tried for pretended offenses:

For abolishing the free system of English laws in a neighbouring province, establishing therein an arbitrary government, and enlarging its boundaries so as to render it at once an example and fit instrument for introducing the same absolute rule into these colonies:

For taking away our charters, abolishing our most valuable laws, and altering fundamentally the forms of our governments:

For suspending our own legislatures, and declaring themselves invested with power to legislate for us in all cases whatsoever.

He has abdicated government here, by declaring us out of his protection and waging war against us.

He has plundered our seas, ravaged our coasts, burnt our towns, and destroyed the lives of our people.

He is at this time transporting large armies of foreign mercenaries to complete the works of death, desolation and tyranny, already begun with circumstances of cruelty and perfidy scarcely paralleled in the most barbarous ages, and totally unworthy the head of a civilized nation.

He has constrained our fellow citizens taken captive on the high seas to bear arms against their country, to become the executioners of their friends and brethren, or to fall themselves by their hands.

He has excited domestic insurrections amongst us, and has endeavoured to bring on the inhabitants of our frontiers, the merciless Indian savages, whose known rule of warfare is an undistinguished destruction of all ages, sexes and conditions.

In every stage of these oppressions we have petitioned for redress in the most humble terms: Our repeated petitions have been answered only by repeated injury. A prince, whose character is thus marked by every act which may define a tyrant, is unfit to be the ruler of a free people.

Nor have we been wanting in attentions to our British brethren. We have warned them from time to time of attempts by their legislature to extend an unwarrantable jurisdiction over us. We have reminded them of the circumstances of our emigration and settlement here. We have appealed to their native justice and magnanimity, and we have conjured them by the ties of our common kindred to disavow these usurpations, which, would inevitably interrupt our connections and correspondence. They too have been deaf to the voice of justice and of consanguinity. We must, therefore, acquiesce in the necessity which denounces our separation, and hold them, as we hold the rest of mankind, enemies in war, in peace friends.

WE, THEREFORE, the Representatives of the United States of America, in General Congress, Assembled, appealing to the Supreme Judge of the world for the rectitude of our intentions, do, in the name, and by authority of the good people of these Colonies, solemnly publish and declare, That these United Colonies are, and of right ought to be FREE AND INDEPENDENT STATES; that they are absolved from all allegiance to the British Crown, and that all political connection between them and the State of Great Britain, is and ought to be totally dissolved; and that as free and independent States, they have full power to levy war, conclude peace, contract alliances, establish commerce, and to do all other acts and things which independent States may of right do. And for the support of this Declaration, with a firm reliance on the protection of Divine Providence, we mutually pledge to each other our lives, our fortunes and our sacred honor.

JOHN HANCOCK.

New Hampshire

JOSIAH BARTLETT   MATTHEW THORNTON
WM. WHIPPLE

Massachusetts Bay

SAML. ADAMS   ROBT. TREAT PAINE
JOHN ADAMS   ELBRIDGE GERRY

Rhode Island

STEP. HOPKINS   WILLIAM ELLERY

Connecticut

ROGER SHERMAN   WM. WILLIAMS
SAML. HUNTINGTON   OLIVER WOLCOTT

New York

WM. FLOYD   FRANS. LEWIS
PHIL. LIVINGSTON   LEWIS MORRIS

New Jersey

RICHD. STOCKTON   JOHN HART
JNO. WITHERSPOON   ABRA. CLARK
FRAS. HOPKINSON

Pennsylvania

ROBT. MORRIS
BENJAMIN RUSH
BENJA. FRANKLIN
JOHN MORTON
GEO. CLYMER

JAS. SMITH
GEO. TAYLOR
JAMES WILSON
GEO. ROSS

Delaware

CAESAR RODNEY
GEO. READ

THO. M'KEAN

Maryland

SAMUEL CHASE
WM. PACA
THOS. STONE

CHARLES CARROLL
of Carrollton

Virginia

GEORGE WYTHE
RICHARD HENRY LEE
TH. JEFFERSON
BENJA. HARRISON

THOS. NELSON JR.
FRANCIS LIGHTFOOT LEE
CARTER BRAXTON

North Carolina

WM. HOOPER
JOSEPH HEWES

JOHN PENN

South Carolina

EDWARD RUTLEDGE.
THOS. HEYWARD JUNR.

THOMAS LYNCH JUNR.
ARTHUR MIDDLETON

Georgia

BUTTON GWINNETT
LYMAN HALL

GEO. WALTON.

CONSTITUTION OF THE UNITED STATES OF AMERICA

PREAMBLE

WE THE PEOPLE of the United States, in order to form a more perfect Union, establish justice, insure domestic tranquility, provide for the common defense, promote the general welfare, and secure the blessings of liberty to ourselves and our posterity, do ordain and establish this Constitution for the United States of America.

ARTICLE I

SECTION 1. All legislative powers herein granted shall be vested in a Congress of the United States, which shall consist of a Senate and House of Representatives.

SECTION 2. The House of Representatives shall be composed of members chosen every second year by the people of the several States, and the electors in each State shall have the qualifications requisite for electors of the most numerous branch of the State Legislature.

No person shall be a representative who shall not have attained to the age of twenty-five years, and been seven years a citizen of the United States, and who shall not, when elected, be an inhabitant of that State in which he shall be chosen.

Representatives and direct taxes shall be apportioned among the several States which may be included within this Union, according to their respective numbers, which shall be determined by adding to the whole number of free persons, including those bound to service for a term of years, and excluding Indians not taxed, three-fifths of all other persons. The actual enumeration shall be made within three years after the first meeting of the Congress of the United States, and within every subsequent term of ten years, in such manner as they shall by law direct. The number of representatives shall not exceed one for every thirty thousand, but each State shall have at least one representative; and until such enumeration shall be made, the State of New Hampshire shall be entitled to choose three, Massachusetts eight, Rhode Island and Providence Plantations one, Connecticut five, New York six, New Jersey four, Pennsylvania eight, Delaware one, Maryland six, Virginia ten, North Carolina five, South Carolina five, and Georgia three.

When vacancies happen in the representation from any State, the Executive authority thereof shall issue writs of election to fill such vacancies.

The House of Representatives shall choose their Speaker and other officers; and shall have the sole power of impeachment.

SECTION 3. The Senate of the United States shall be composed of two senators from each State, chosen by the legislature thereof, for six years and each senator shall have one vote.

Immediately after they shall be assembled in consequence of the first election, they shall be divided as equally as may be into three classes. The seats of the senators of the first class shall be vacated at the expiration of the second year, of the second class at the expiration of the fourth year, and of the third class at the expiration of the sixth year, so that one-third may be chosen every second year; and if vacancies happen by resignation, or otherwise, during the recess of the legislature of any State, the executive thereof may make temporary appointments until the next meeting of the legislature, which shall then fill such vacancies.

No person shall be a senator who shall not have attained to the age of thirty years, and been nine years a citizen of the United States, and who shall not, when elected, be an inhabitant of that State for which he shall be chosen.

The Vice President of the United States shall be President of the Senate, but shall have no vote, unless they be equally divided.

The Senate shall choose their other officers, and also a President pro tempore, in the absence of the Vice President, or when he shall exercise the office of President of the United States.

The Senate shall have the sole power to try all impeachments. When sitting for that purpose, they shall be on oath or affirmation. When the President of the United States is tried, the Chief Justice shall preside: And no person shall be convicted without the concurrence of two thirds of the members present.

Judgment in cases of impeachment shall not extend further than to removal from office, and disqualification to hold and enjoy any office or honor, trust or profit under the United States: but the party convicted shall nevertheless be liable and subject to indictment, trial, judgment and punishment, according to law.

SECTION 4. The times, places and manner of holding elections for senators and representatives, shall be prescribed in each State by the legislature thereof; but the Congress may at any time by law make or alter such regulations, except as to the places of choosing senators.

The Congress shall assemble at least once in every year, and such meeting shall be on the first Monday in December, unless they shall by law appoint a different day.

SECTION 5. Each house shall be the judge of the elections, returns and qualifications of its own members, and a majority of each shall constitute a quorum to do business; but a smaller number may adjourn from day to day, and may be authorized to compel the attendance of absent members, in such manner, and under such penalties as each house may provide.

Each house may determine the rules of its proceedings, punish its members for disorderly behaviour, and, with the concurrence of two-thirds, expel a member.

Each house shall keep a journal of its proceedings, and from time to time publish the same, excepting such parts as may in their judgment require secrecy; and the yeas and the nays of the members of either house on any question shall, at the desire of one-fifth of those present, be entered on the journal.

Neither house, during the session of Congress, shall, without the consent of the other, adjourn for more than three days, nor to any other place than that in which the two houses shall be sitting.

SECTION 6. The senators and representatives shall receive a compensation for their services, to be ascertained by law, and paid out of the Treasury of the United States. They shall in all cases, except treason, felony and breach of the peace, be privileged from arrest during their attendance at the session of their respective houses, and in going to and returning from the same; and for any speech or debate in either house, they shall not be questioned in any other place.

No senator or representative shall, during the time for which he was elected, be appointed to any civil office under the authority of the United States, which shall have been created, or the emoluments whereof shall have been increased during such time; and no person holding any office under the United States, shall be a member of either house during his continuance in office.

SECTION 7. All bills for raising revenue shall originate in the House of Representatives; but the Senate may propose or concur with amendments as on other bills.

Every bill which shall have passed the House of Representatives and the Senate, shall, before it become a law, be presented to the President of the United States; if he approves he shall sign it, but if not he shall return it, with his objections to that house in which it shall have originated, who shall enter the objections at large on their journal, and proceed to reconsider it. If after such reconsideration two thirds of that House shall agree to pass the bill, it shall be sent, together with the objections, to the other House, by which it shall likewise be reconsidered, and if approved by two thirds of that House, it shall become a law. But in all such cases the votes of both Houses shall be determined by yeas and nays, and the names of the persons voting for and against the bill shall be entered on the journal of each House respectively. If any bill shall not be returned by the President within ten days (Sundays excepted) after it shall have been presented to him, the same shall be a law, in like manner as if he had signed it, unless the Congress by their adjournment prevent its return, in which case it shall not be a law.

Every order, resolution, or vote to which the concurrence of the Senate and House of Representatives may be necessary (except on a question of adjournment) shall be presented to the President of the United States; and before the same shall take effect, shall be approved by him, or being disapproved by him, shall be repassed by two thirds of the Senate and House of Representatives, according to the rules and limitations prescribed in the case of a bill.

SECTION 8. The Congress shall have power to lay and collect taxes, duties, imposts and excises, to pay the debts and provide for the common defense and general welfare of the United States; but all duties, imposts and excises shall be uniform throughout the United States;

To borrow money on the credit of the United States;

To regulate commerce with foreign nations, and among the several States, and with the Indian tribes;

To establish a uniform rule of naturalization, and uniform laws on the subject of bankruptcies throughout the United States;

To coin money, regulate the value thereof, and of foreign coin, and fix the standard of weights and measures;

To provide for the punishment of counterfeiting the securities and current coin of the United States;

To establish post offices and post roads;

To promote the progress of science and useful arts, by securing for limited times to authors and inventors the exclusive right to their respective writings and discoveries;

To constitute tribunals inferior to the Supreme Court;

To define and punish piracies and felonies committed on the high seas, and offenses against the law of nations;

To declare war, grant letters of marque and reprisal, and make rules concerning captures on land and water;

To raise and support armies, but no appropriation of money to that use shall be for a longer term than two years;

To provide and maintain a Navy;

To make rules for the government and regulation of the land and naval forces;

To provide for calling forth the militia to execute the laws of the Union, suppress insurrections and repel invasions;

To provide for organizing, arming, and disciplining the militia, and for governing such part of them as may be employed in the service of the United States, reserving to the States respectively, the appointment of the officers, and the authority of training the militia according to the discipline prescribed by Congress;

To exercise exclusive legislation in all cases whatsoever, over such district (not exceeding ten miles square) as may, by cession of particular States, and the acceptance of Congress, become the seat of the Government of the United States, and to exercise like authority over all places purchased by the consent of the legislature of the State in which the same shall be, for the erection of forts, magazines, arsenals, dock-yards, and other needful buildings;—And

To make all laws which shall be necessary and proper for carrying into execution the foregoing powers and all other powers vested by this Constitution in the Government of the United States, or in any department or officer thereof.

SECTION 9. The migration or importation of such persons as any of the States now existing shall think proper to admit, shall not be prohibited by the Congress prior to the year one thousand eight hundred and eight, but a tax or duty may be imposed on such importation, not exceeding ten dollars for each person.

The privilege of the writ of habeas corpus shall not be suspended, unless when in cases of rebellion or invasion the public safety may require it.

No bill of attainder or ex post facto law shall be passed.

No capitation, or other direct, tax shall be laid, unless in proportion to the census or enumeration herein before directed to be taken.

No tax or duty shall be laid on articles exported from any State.

No preference shall be given by any regulation of commerce or revenue to the ports of one State over those of another: nor shall vessels bound to, or from, one State, be obliged to enter, clear, or pay duties in another.

No money shall be drawn from the Treasury, but in consequence of appropriations made by law; and a regular statement and account of the receipts and expenditures of all public money shall be published from time to time.

No title of nobility shall be granted by the United States: And no person holding any office of profit or trust under them, shall, without the consent of the Congress, accept of any present, emolument, office, or title, of any kind whatever, from any King, Prince, or foreign State.

Section 10. No State shall enter into any treaty, alliance, or confederation; grant letters of marque and reprisal; coin money; emit bills of credit; make any thing but gold and silver coin a tender in payment of debts; pass any bill of attainder, ex post facto law, or law impairing the obligation of contracts, or grant any title of nobility.

No State shall, without the consent of the Congress, lay any imposts or duties on imports or exports, except what may be absolutely necessary for executing its inspection laws: and the net produce of all duties and imposts, laid by any State on imports or exports, shall be for the use of the Treasury of the United States; and all such laws shall be subject to the revision and control of the Congress.

No State shall, without the consent of Congress, lay any duty of tonnage, keep troops, or ships of war in time of peace, enter into any agreement or compact with another State, or with a foreign power, or engage in war, unless actually invaded, or in such imminent danger as will not admit of delay.

Article II

Section 1. The executive power shall be vested in a President of the United States of America. He shall hold his office during the term of four years, and, together with the Vice President, chosen for the same term, be elected, as follows:

Each State, shall appoint, in such manner as the legislature thereof may direct, a number of electors, equal to the whole number of senators and representatives to which the State may be entitled in the Congress; but no senator or representative, or person holding an office of trust or profit under the United States, shall be appointed an elector.

The electors shall meet in their respective States, and vote by ballot for two persons, of whom one at least shall not be an inhabitant of the same State with themselves. And they shall make a list of all the persons voted for, and of the number of votes for each; which list they shall sign and certify, and transmit sealed to the seat of the Government of the United States, directed to the President of the Senate. The President of the Senate shall, in the presence of the Senate and

House of Representatives, open all the certificates, and the votes shall then be counted. The person having the greatest number of votes shall be the President, if such number be a majority of the whole number of electors appointed; and if there be more than one who have such majority, and have an equal number of votes, then the House of Representatives shall immediately choose by ballot one of them for President; and if no person have a majority, then from the five highest on the list the said House shall in like manner choose the President. But in choosing the President, the votes shall be taken by States, the representation from each State having one vote; a quorum for this purpose shall consist of a member or members from two thirds of the States, and a majority of all the States shall be necessary to a choice. In every case, after the choice of the President, the person having the greatest number of votes of the electors shall be the Vice President. But if there should remain two or more who have equal votes, the Senate shall choose from them by ballot the Vice President.

The Congress may determine the time of choosing the electors, and the day on which they shall give their votes; which day shall be the same throughout the United States.

No person except a natural born citizen, or a citizen of the United States, at the time of the adoption of this Constitution, shall be eligible to the office of President; neither shall any person be eligible to that office who shall not have attained to the age of thirty-five years, and been fourteen years a resident within the United States.

In case of the removal of the President from office, or of his death, resignation, or inability to discharge the powers and duties of the said office, the same shall devolve on the Vice President, and the Congress may by law provide for the case of removal, death, resignation, or inability, both of the President and Vice President, declaring what officer shall then act as President, and such officer shall act accordingly, until the disability be removed, or a President shall be elected.

The President shall, at stated times, receive for his services, a compensation, which shall neither be increased nor diminished during the period for which he shall have been elected, and he shall not receive within that period any other emolument from the United States, or any of them.

Before he enter on the execution of his office, he shall take the following oath or affirmation:—"I do solemnly swear (or affirm) that I will faithfully execute the office of President of the United States, and will to the best of my ability, preserve, protect and defend the Constitution of the United States."

SECTION 2. The President shall be Commander in Chief of the Army and Navy of the United States, and of the militia of the several States, when called into the actual service of the United States; he may require the opinion, in writing, of the principal officer in each of the Executive Departments, upon any subject relating to the duties of their respective offices, and he shall have power to grant reprieves and pardons for offenses against the United States, except in cases of impeachment.

He shall have power, by and with the advice and consent of the Senate, to make treaties, provided two thirds of the Senators present concur; and he shall nominate, and by and with the advice and consent of the Senate, shall appoint ambassadors, other public ministers and consuls, Judges of the Supreme Court, and all other officers of the United States, whose appointments are not herein otherwise provided for, and which shall be established by law: but the Congress may by law vest the appointment of such inferior officers, as they think proper, in the President alone, in the courts of law, or in the heads of departments.

The President shall have power to fill up all vacancies that may happen during the recess of the Senate, by granting commissions which shall expire at the end of their next session.

SECTION 3. He shall from time to time give to the Congress information of the state of the Union, and recommend to their consideration such measures as he shall judge necessary and expedient; he may, on extraordinary occasions, convene both houses, or either of them, and in case of disagreement between them, with respect to the time of adjournment, he may adjourn them to such time as he shall think proper; he shall receive ambassadors and other public ministers; he shall take care that the laws be faithfully executed, and shall commission all the officers of the United States.

SECTION 4. The President, Vice President and all civil officers of the United States, shall be removed from office on impeachment for, and conviction of, treason, bribery, or other high crimes and misdemeanors.

ARTICLE III

SECTION 1. The judicial power of the United States, shall be vested in one Supreme Court, and in such inferior courts as the Congress may from time to time ordain and establish. The judges, both of the supreme and inferior courts, shall hold their offices during good behaviour, and shall, at stated times, receive for their services, a compensation, which shall not be diminished during their continuance in office.

SECTION 2. The judicial power shall extend to all cases, in law and equity, arising under this Constitution, the laws of the United States, and treaties made, or which shall be made, under their authority;—to all cases affecting ambassadors, other public ministers and consuls;—to all cases of admiralty and maritime jurisdiction;—to controversies to which the United States shall be a party;—to controversies between two or more States;—between a State and citizens of another State;—between citizens of different States,—between citizens of the same State claiming lands under grants of different States, and between a State, or the citizens thereof, and foreign States, citizens or subjects.

In all cases affecting ambassadors, other public ministers and consuls, and those in which a State shall be a party, the Supreme Court shall have original jurisdiction. In all the other cases before mentioned, the Supreme Court shall have appellate jurisdiction, both as to law and fact, with such exceptions, and under such regulations as the Congress shall make.

The trial of all crimes, except in cases of impeachment, shall be by jury; and such trial shall be held in the State where the said crimes shall have been committed; but when not committed within any State, the trial shall be at such place or places as the Congress may by law have directed.

SECTION 3. Treason against the United States, shall consist only in levying war against them, or in adhering to their enemies, giving them aid and comfort. No person shall be convicted of treason unless on the testimony of two witnesses to the same overt act, or on confession in open court.

The Congress shall have power to declare the punishment of treason, but no attainder of treason shall work corruption of blood, or forfeiture except during the life of the person attainted.

ARTICLE IV

SECTION 1. Full faith and credit shall be given in each State to the public acts, records, and judicial proceedings of every other State. And the Congress may by general laws prescribe the manner in which such acts, records and proceedings shall be proved, and the effect thereof.

SECTION 2. The citizens of each State shall be entitled to all privileges and immunities of citizens in the several States.

A person charged in any State with treason, felony, or other crime, who shall flee from justice, and be found in another State, shall on demand of the executive authority of the State from which he fled, be delivered up, to be removed to the State having jurisdiction of the crime.

No person held to service or labour in one State, under the laws thereof, escaping into another, shall, in consequence of any law or regulation therein, be discharged from such service or labour, but shall be delivered up on claim of the party to whom such service or labour may be due.

SECTION 3. New States may be admitted by the Congress into this Union; but no new State shall be formed or erected within the jurisdiction of any other State; nor any State be formed by the junction of two or more States, or parts of States, without the consent of the legislatures of the States concerned as well as of the Congress.

The Congress shall have power to dispose of and make all needful rules and regulations respecting the Territory or other property belonging to the United States; and nothing in this Consitution shall be so construed as to prejudice any claims of the United States, or of any particular State.

SECTION 4. The United States shall guarantee to every State in this Union a republican form of Government, and shall protect each of them against invasion; and on application of the legislature, or of the executive (when the legislature cannot be convened) against domestic violence.

ARTICLE V

The Congress, whenever two third of both Houses shall deem it necessary, shall propose amendments to this Constitution, or on the application of the legislatures of two thirds of the several States, shall call a convention for proposing amendments, which, in either case, shall be valid to all intents and purposes, as part of this Constitution, when ratified by the legislatures of three fourths of the several States, or by conventions in three fourths thereof, as the one or the other mode of ratification may be proposed by the Congress; provided that no amendment which may be made prior to the year one thousand eight hundred and eight shall in any manner affect the first and fourth clauses in the Ninth Section of the First Article; and that no State, without its consent, shall be deprived of its equal suffrage in the Senate.

ARTICLE VI

All debts contracted and engagements entered into, before the adoption of this Constitution, shall be as valid against the United States under this Constitution, as under the Confederation.

This Constitution, and the laws of the United States which shall be made in pursuance thereof; and all treaties made, or which shall be made, under the authority of the United States, shall be the supreme law of the land; and the judges in every State shall be bound thereby, any thing in the Constitution or laws of any State to the contrary notwithstanding.

The senators and representatives before mentioned, and the members of the several State legislatures, and all executive and judicial officers, both of the United States and of the several States, shall be bound by oath or affirmation, to support this Constitution; but no religious test shall ever be required as a qualification to any office or public trust under the United States.

ARTICLE VII

The ratification of the conventions of nine States shall be sufficient for the establishment of this Constitution between the States so ratifying the same.

Done in convention by the unanimous consent of the States present the seventeenth day of September in the year of our Lord one thousand seven hundred and eighty seven and of the Independence of the United States of America the twelfth. In witness whereof we have hereunto subscribed our names,

Go. WASHINGTON—*Presid't.*
and deputy from Virginia

Attest WILLIAM JACKSON *Secretary*

New Hampshire

JOHN LANGDON   NICHOLAS GILMAN

Massachusetts

NATHANIEL GORHAM   RUFUS KING

Connecticut

WM. SAML. JOHNSON   ROGER SHERMAN

New York

ALEXANDER HAMILTON

New Jersey

WIL: LIVINGSTON   WM. PATERSON
DAVID BREARLEY   JONA: DAYTON

Pennsylvania

B. FRANKLIN

THOMAS MIFFLIN

ROBT. MORRIS

GEO. CLYMER

THOS. FITZSIMONS

JARED INGERSOLL

JAMES WILSON

GOUV. MORRIS

Delaware

GEO: READ

GUNNING BEDFORD JUN

JOHN DICKINSON

RICHARD BASSETT

JACO: BROOM

Maryland

JAMES MCHENRY

DAN. OF ST. THOS. JENIFER

DANL. CARROLL

Virginia

JOHN BLAIR—

JAMES MADISON JR.

North Carolina

WM. BLOUNT

RICHD. DOBBS SPAIGHT

HU. WILLIAMSON

South Carolina

J. RUTLEDGE

CHARLES COTESWORTH
  PINCKNEY

CHARLES PINCKNEY

PIERCE BUTLER

Georgia

WILLIAM FEW

ABR. BALDWIN

AMENDMENTS

ARTICLE I

Congress shall make no law respecting an establishment of religion, or prohibiting the free exercise thereof; or abridging the freedom of speech, or of the press; or the right of the people peaceably to assemble, and to petition the Government for a redress of grievances.

ARTICLE II

A well regulated militia, being necessary to the security of a free State, the right of the people to keep and bear arms, shall not be infringed.

ARTICLE III

No soldier shall, in time of peace be quartered in any house, without the consent of the owner, nor in time of war, but in a manner to be prescribed by law.

ARTICLE IV

The right of the people to be secure in their persons, houses, papers, and effects, against unreasonable searches and seizures, shall not be violated, and no warrants shall issue, but upon probable cause, supported by oath or affirmation, and particularly describing the place to be searched, and the persons or things to be seized.

ARTICLE V

No person shall be held to answer for a capital, or otherwise infamous crime, unless on a presentment or indictment of a Grand Jury, except in cases arising in the land of naval forces, or in the militia, when in actual service in time of war or public danger; nor shall any person be subject for the same offense to be twice put in jeopardy of life or limb; nor shall be compelled in any criminal case to be a witness against himself, nor be deprived of life, liberty, or property, without due process of law; nor shall private property be taken for public use, without just compensation.

ARTICLE VI

In all criminal prosecutions, the accused shall enjoy the right to a speedy and public trial, by an impartial jury of the State and district wherein the crime shall have been committed, which district shall have been previously ascertained by law, and to be informed of the nature and cause of the accusation; to be confronted with the witnesses against him; to have compulsory process for obtaining witnesses in his favor, and to have the assistance of counsel for his defense.

ARTICLE VII

In suits at common law, where the value in controversy shall exceed twenty dollars, the right of trial by jury shall be preserved, and no fact tried by a jury, shall be otherwise reexamined in any court of the United States, than according to the rules of the common law.

ARTICLE VIII

Excessive bail shall not be required, nor excessive fines imposed, nor cruel and unusual punishments inflicted.

ARTICLE IX

The enumeration in the Constitution, of certain rights, shall not be construed to deny or disparage others retained by the people.

ARTICLE X

The powers not delegated to the United States by the Constitution, nor prohibited by it to the States, are reserved to the States respectively, or to the people.

ARTICLE XI

The judicial power of the United States shall not be construed to extend to any suit in law or equity, commenced or prosecuted against one of the United States by citizens of another State, or by citizens or subjects of any foreign State.

ARTICLE XII

The electors shall meet in their respective States, and vote by ballot for President and Vice President, one of whom, at least, shall not be an inhabitant of the same State with themselves; they shall name in their ballots the person voted for as President, and in distinct ballots the person voted for as Vice President, and they shall make distinct lists of all persons voted for as President, and of all persons voted for as Vice President, and of the number of votes for each, which lists they shall sign and certify, and transmit sealed to the seat of the government of the United States, directed to the President of the Senate;— The President of the Senate shall, in the presence of the Senate and House of Representatives, open all the certificates and the votes shall then be counted;—The person having the greatest number of votes for President, shall be the President, if such number be a majority of the whole number of electors appointed; and if no person have such majority, then from the persons having the highest numbers not exceeding three on the list of those voted for as President, the House of Representatives shall choose immediately, by ballot, the President. But in choosing the President, the votes shall be taken by States, the representation from each State having one vote; a quorum for this purpose shall consist of a member or members from two-thirds of the States, and a majority of all the States shall be necessary to a choice. And if the House of Representatives shall not choose a President whenever the right of choice shall devolve upon them, before the fourth day of March next following, then the Vice President shall act as President, as in the case of the death or other constitutional disability of the President.—The person having the greatest number of votes as Vice President, shall be the Vice President, if such number be a majority of the whole number of electors appointed, and if no person have a majority, then from the two highest numbers on the list, the Senate shall choose the Vice President; a quorum for the purpose shall consist of two-thirds of the whole number of Senators, and a majority of the whole number shall be necessary to a choice. But no person constitutionally ineligible to the office of President shall be eligible to that of Vice President of the United States.

ARTICLE XIII

SECTION 1. Neither slavery nor involuntary servitude, except as a punishment for crime whereof the party shall have been duly convicted, shall exist within the United States, or any place subject to their jurisdiction.

SECTION 2. Congress shall have power to enforce this article by appropriate legislation.

ARTICLE XIV

SECTION 1. All persons born or naturalized in the United States, and subject to the jurisdiction thereof, are citizens of the United States and of the State wherein they reside. No State shall make or enforce any law which shall abridge the privileges or immunities of citizens of the United States; nor shall any State deprive any person of life, liberty, or property, without due process of law; nor deny to any person within its jurisdiction the equal protection of the laws.

SECTION 2. Representatives shall be apportioned among the several States according to their respective numbers, counting the whole number of persons in each State, excluding Indians not taxed. But when the right to vote at any election for the choice of electors for President and Vice President of the United States, Representatives in Congress, the executive and judicial officers of a State, or the members of the legislature thereof, is denied to any of the male inhabitants of such State, being twenty-one years of age, and citizens of the United States, or in any way abridged, except for participation in rebellion, or other crime, the basis of representation therein shall be reduced in the proportion which the number of such male citizens shall bear to the whole number of male citizens twenty-one years of age in such State.

SECTION 3. No person shall be a Senator or Representative in Congress, or elector of President and Vice President, or hold any office, civil or military, under the United States, or under any State, who, having previously taken an oath, as a member of Congress, or as an officer of the United States, or as a member of any State legislature, or as an executive or judicial officer of any State, to support the Constitution of the United States, shall have engaged in insurrection or rebellion against the same, or given aid or comfort to the enemies thereof. But Congress may by a vote of two-thirds of each house, remove such disability.

SECTION 4. The validity of the public debt of the United States, authorized by law, including debts incurred for payment of pensions and bounties for services in suppressing insurrection or rebellion, shall not be questioned. But neither the United States nor any State shall assume or pay any debt or obligation incurred in aid of insurrection or rebellion against the United States, or any claim for the loss or emancipation of any slave; but all such debts, obligations and claims shall be held illegal and void.

SECTION 5. The Congress shall have power to enforce, by appropriate legislation, the provisions of this article.

ARTICLE XV

SECTION 1. The right of citizens of the United States to vote shall not be denied or abridged by the United States or by any State on account of race, color, or previous condition of servitude.

SECTION 2. The Congress shall have power to enforce this article by appropriate legislation.

ARTICLE XVI

The Congress shall have power to lay and collect taxes on incomes, from whatever source derived, without apportionment among the several States, and without regard to any census or enumeration.

ARTICLE XVII

SECTION 1. The Senate of the United States shall be composed of two senators from each State, elected by the people thereof, for six years; and each senator shall have one vote. The electors in each State shall have the qualifications requisite for electors of the most numerous branch of the State legislatures.

SECTION 2. When vacancies happen in the representation of any State in the senate, the executive authority of such State shall issue writs of election to fill such vacancies: *Provided,* That the legislature of any State may empower the executive thereof to make temporary appointments until the people fill the vacancies by election as the legislature may direct.

SECTION 3. This amendment shall not be so construed as to affect the election or term of any senator chosen before it becomes valid as part of the Constitution.

ARTICLE XVIII

SECTION 1. After one year from the ratification of this article the manufacture, sale, or transportation of intoxicating liquors within, the importation thereof into, or the exportation thereof from the United States and all territory subject to the jurisdiction thereof for beverage purposes is hereby prohibited.

SECTION 2. The Congress and the several States shall have concurrent power to enforce this article by appropriate legislation.

SECTION 3. This article shall be inoperative unless it shall have been ratified as an amendment to the Constitution by the legislatures of the several States, as provided in the Constitution, within seven years from the date of the submission hereof to the States by the Congress.

ARTICLE XIX

SECTION 1. The right of citizens of the United States to vote shall not be denied or abridged by the United States or by any State on account of sex.

SECTION 2. Congress shall have power to enforce this article by appropriate legislation.

ARTICLE XX

SECTION 1. The terms of the President and Vice President shall end at noon on the 20th day of January, and the terms of Senators and Representatives at noon on the 3d day of January, of the years in which such terms would have ended if this article had not been ratified; and the terms of their successors shall then begin.

SECTION 2. The Congress shall assemble at least once in every year, and such meeting shall begin at noon on the 3d day of January, unless they shall by law appoint a different day.

SECTION 3. If, at the time fixed for the beginning of the term of the President, the President elect shall have died, the Vice President elect shall become President. If a President shall not have been chosen before the time fixed for the beginning of his term, or if the President elect shall have failed to qualify, then the Vice President elect shall act as President until a President shall have qualified; and the Congress may by law provide for the case wherein neither a President elect nor a Vice President elect shall have qualified, declaring who shall then act as President, or the manner in which one who is to act shall be selected, and such person shall act accordingly until a President or Vice President shall have qualified.

SECTION 4. The Congress may by law provide for the case of the death of any of the persons from whom the House of Representatives may choose a President whenever the right of choice shall have devolved upon them, and for the case of the death of any of the persons from whom the Senate may choose a Vice President whenever the right of choice shall have devolved upon them.

SECTION 5. Sections 1 and 2 shall take effect on the 15th day of October following the ratification of this article.

SECTION 6. This article shall be inoperative unless it shall have been ratified as an amendment to the Constitution by the legislatures of three-fourths of the several States within seven years from the date of its submission.

ARTICLE XXI

SECTION 1. The eighteenth article of amendment to the Constitution of the United States is hereby repealed.

SECTION 2. The transportation or importation into any State, Territory, or possession of the United States for delivery or use therein of intoxicating liquors, in violation of the laws thereof, is hereby prohibited.

SECTION 3. This article shall be inoperative unless it shall have been ratified as an amendment to the Constitution by conventions in the several States, as provided in the Constitution, within seven years from the date of the submission hereof to the States by the Congress.

ARTICLE XXII

SECTION 1. No person shall be elected to the office of the President more than twice, and no person who has held the office of President, or acted as President, for more than 2 years of a term to which some other person was elected President shall be elected to the office of the President more than once. But this Article shall not apply to any person holding the office of President when this Article was proposed by the Congress, and shall not prevent any person who may be holding the office of President, or acting as President, during the term within which this Article becomes operative from holding the office of President or acting as President during the remainder of such term.

SECTION 2. This Article shall be inoperative unless it shall have been ratified as an amendment to the Constitution by the legislatures of three-fourths of the several States within 7 years from the date of its submission to the States by the Congress.

ARTICLE XXIII

SECTION 1. The District constituting the seat of Government of the United States shall appoint in such manner as the Congress may direct:

A number of electors of President and Vice President equal to the whole number of Senators and Representatives in Congress to which the District would be entitled if it were a State, but in no event more than the least populous State; they shall be in addition to those appointed by the States, but they shall be considered, for the purposes of the election of President and Vice President, to be electors appointed by a State; and they shall meet in the District and perform such duties as provided by the twelfth article of amendment.

SECTION 2. The Congress shall have power to enforce this article by appropriate legislation.

ARTICLE XXIV

SECTION 1. The right of citizens of the United States to vote in any primary or other election for President or Vice President, for electors for President or Vice President, or for Senator or Representative in Congress, shall not be denied or abridged by the United States or any State by reason of failure to pay any poll tax or other tax.

SECTION 2. The Congress shall have power to enforce this article by appropriate legislation.

ARTICLE XXV

SECTION 1. In case of the removal of the President from office or of his death or resignation, the Vice President shall become President.

SECTION 2. Whenever there is a vacancy in the office of the Vice President, the President shall nominate a Vice President who shall take office upon confirmation by a majority vote of both Houses of Congress.

SECTION 3. Whenever the President transmits to the President pro tempore of the Senate and the Speaker of the House of Representatives his written declaration that he is unable to discharge the powers and duties of his office, and until he transmits to them a written declaration to the contrary, such powers and duties shall be discharged by the Vice President as Acting President.

SECTION 4. Whenever the Vice President and a majority of either the principal officers of the executive departments or of such other body as Congress may by law provide, transmit to the President pro tempore of the Senate and the Speaker of the House of Representatives their written declaration that the President is unable to discharge the powers and duties of his office, the Vice President shall immediately assume the powers and duties of the office as Acting President.

Thereafter, when the President transmits to the President pro tempore of the Senate and the Speaker of the House of Representatives his written declaration that no inability exists, he shall resume the powers and duties of his office unless the Vice President and a majority of either the principal officers of the executive department or of such other body as Congress may by law provide, transmit within four days to the President pro tempore of the Senate and the Speaker of the House of Representatives their written declaration that the President is unable to discharge the powers and duties of his office. Thereupon Congress shall decide the issue, assembling within forty-eight hours for that purpose if not in session. If the Congress, within twenty-one days after receipt of the latter written declaration, or if Congress is not in session, within twenty-one days after Congress is required to assemble, determines by two-thirds vote of both Houses that the President is unable to discharge the powers and duties of his office, the Vice President shall continue to discharge the same as Acting President; otherwise, the President shall resume the powers and duties of his office.

DISTRICT OFFICES

Immigration and Naturalization Service

Alaska
U.S. Post Office & Courthouse
Building, Room 143
Anchorage, Alaska 99501
Arizona
230 North First Avenue
Phoenix, Arizona 85025
California
300 North Los Angeles Street
Los Angeles, California 90012

Appraisers Building,
630 Sansome Street
San Francisco, California 94111
Colorado
17027 Federal Office Building
Denver, Colorado 80202
Connecticut
135 High Street,
P.O. Box 1724
Hartford, Connecticut 06101
Florida
Room 1402, Federal Building
51 S.W. First Avenue
Miami, Florida 33130
Georgia
881 Peachtree Street, N.E.
Atlanta, Georgia 30309
Hawaii
595 Ala Moana Boulevard
P.O. Box 461
Honolulu, Hawaii 96809

Illinois
Courthouse & Federal
Office Building
219 South Dearborn Street
Chicago, Illinois 60604
Louisiana
New Federal Building
701 Loyola Avenue
New Orleans, Louisiana 70113
Maine
319 U.S. Courthouse,
P.O. Box 578
Portland, Maine 04112
Maryland
707 North Calvert Street
Baltimore, Maryland 21202
Massachusetts
150 Tremont Street
Boston, Massachusetts 02111
Michigan
Federal Building
333 Mount Elliott Street
Detroit, Michigan 48207
Minnesota
1014 New Post Office Building
180 E. Kellogg Boulevard
St. Paul, Minnesota 55101
Missouri
819 U.S. Courthouse
811 Grand Avenue
Kansas City, Missouri 64106

129

Montana
  Federal Building,
  P.O. Box 1724
  Helena, Montana 59601
Nebraska
  New Federal Building
  215 North 17th Street
  Omaha, Nebraska 68102
New Jersey
  1060 Broad Street
  Newark, New Jersey 07102
New York
  68 Court Street
  Buffalo, New York 14202

  20 West Broadway
  New York, New York 10007
Ohio
  600 Standard Building
  1370 Ontario Street
  Cleveland, Ohio 44113
Oregon
  333 U.S. Courthouse
  Broadway & Main Streets
  Portland, Oregon 97205
Pennsylvania
  128 North Broad Street
  Philadelphia, Pennsylvania 19102

Puerto Rico
  804 Ponce de Leon Avenue
  Santurce, Puerto Rico 00908
  San Juan, Puerto Rico

Texas
  343 U.S. Courthouse,
  P.O. Box 9398
  El Paso, Texas 79984

  Route 3
  Los Fresnos, Texas
  Port Isabel, Texas 78566

  U.S. Post Office & Courthouse
  P.O. Box 2539
  San Antonio, Texas 78206

Vermont
  45 Kingman Street
  St. Albans, Vermont 05478

Washington, D.C.
  1025 Vermont Avenue, N.W.
  Washington, D.C. 20536

Washington
  815 Airport Way, S.
  Seattle, Washington 98134

Form approved.
Budget Bureau No. 43–R079.9

UNITED STATES DEPARTMENT OF JUSTICE
IMMIGRATION AND NATURALIZATION SERVICE

Mail or take to:
IMMIGRATION AND NATURALIZATION SERVICE

ALIEN REGISTRATION
(Show the exact spelling of your name as it appears on your alien registration receipt card, and the number of your card. If you did not register, so state.)
Name ....
No. ....

APPLICATION TO FILE PETITION FOR NATURALIZATION

(See INSTRUCTIONS, page 5. BE SURE YOU UNDERSTAND EACH QUESTION BEFORE YOU ANSWER IT.)

I desire to file a petition for naturalization in the—   Date: ....

.... Court at ....
　　　　(Name of Court)　　　　　　　　　　　　　　(City)　　　　　　　　　　　　(State)

My name is: ....
　　　　　　　　　　(Print or type here your present full name only)

I live at: ....
　　　　　(Print or type present apartment number, street address, and if appropriate "in care of")

....
　　　(City)　　　　　　　　　　　　(County)　　　　　　　(State)　(ZIP Code)

Other names I have used are: ....
　　　　　　　　　　　　(Print or type here any other name you have ever used, including maiden name)

My present occupation is .... Sex: ☐ Male ☐ Female

(1a) Was your father or mother ever a United States citizen? (If "Yes" explain fully separately) .... ☐ Yes ☐ No
(1b) Can you read and write English? .... ☐ Yes ☐ No
(1c) Can you speak English? .... ☐ Yes ☐ No
(1d) Can you sign your name in English? .... ☐ Yes ☐ No
(2) In what places in the United States have you lived during the last 5 years? List present address FIRST.

FROM—	TO—	STREET ADDRESS	CITY AND STATE
(a) .... , 19	PRESENT TIME		
(b) .... , 19	.... , 19		
(c) .... , 19	.... , 19		
(d) .... , 19	.... , 19		
(e) .... , 19	.... , 19		

(3) What were the names, addresses, and occupations (or types of business) of your employers during the last 5 years? (If none, write "None.")
List present employment FIRST.

FROM—	TO—	EMPLOYER'S NAME	ADDRESS	OCCUPATION OR TYPE OF BUSINESS
(a) .... , 19	PRESENT TIME			
(b) .... , 19	.... , 19			
(c) .... , 19	.... , 19			
(d) .... , 19	.... , 19			

(4) Have you been out of the United States since you first arrived? .... ☐ Yes ☐ No
If "Yes" fill in the following information for every absence of *less than 6 months*, no matter how short it was.

DATE DEPARTED	DATE RETURNED	NAME OF SHIP, OR OF AIRLINE, RAILROAD COMPANY, BUS COMPANY, OR OTHER MEANS USED TO RETURN TO THE UNITED STATES	PLACE OR PORT OF ENTRY THROUGH WHICH YOU RETURNED TO THE UNITED STATES
....	....		
....	....		
....	....		
....	....		

(5) How many times have you been married? ...... How many times has your husband or wife been married? ...... If either of you has been
married more than once, fill in the following information for each previous marriage.

DATE MARRIED	DATE MARRIAGE ENDED	NAME OF PERSON TO WHOM MARRIED	SEX	(Check one) PERSON MARRIED WAS CITIZEN ☐ ALIEN ☐	HOW MARRIAGE ENDED
(a)				☐ ...... ☐	
(b)				☐ ...... ☐	
(c)				☐ ...... ☐	
(d)				☐ ...... ☐	

(6) The law provides that you may not be regarded as qualified for naturalization under certain conditions, if you knowingly committed certain offenses or crimes, even though you may not have been arrested therefor. Have you ever, in or outside the United States:

    (a) Knowingly committed any crime for which you have not been arrested?..☐ Yes ☐ No

    (b) been arrested, charged, indicted, convicted, fined or imprisoned for breaking or violating any law or ordnance, including

    traffic regulations?..☐ Yes ☐ No

If you answer "Yes" to *(a)* or *(b)*, give the following information as to each incident.

	When	Where	(City)	(State)	(Country)	Nature of Offense	Outcome of Case, If Any
(a)							
(b)							
(c)							
(d)							
(e)							

(7) List your present and past membership in every organization, association, fund, foundation, party, club, society, or similar group in the United States and in any other place, and your foreign military service. (If none, write "None."

(a) _____ , 19 _____ to 19 _____

(b) _____ , 19 _____ to 19 _____

(c) _____ , 19 _____ to 19 _____

(d) _____ , 19 _____ to 19 _____

(e) _____ , 19 _____ to 19 _____

(f) _____ , 19 _____ to 19 _____

(g) _____ , 19 _____ to 19 _____

(8) *(a)* Are you now, or have you ever, in the United States or in any other place, been a member of, or in any other way connected or associated with the Communist Party?...☐ Yes ☐ No

    (b) Have you ever knowingly aided or supported the Communist Party directly, or indirectly through another organization, group, or person?...☐ Yes ☐ No

    (c) Do you now or have you ever advocated, taught, believed in, or knowingly supported or furthered the interests of, Communism?...☐ Yes ☐ No

(9) Have you borne any hereditary title or have you been of any order of nobility in any foreign state?.......................☐ Yes ☐ No

(10) Have you ever been a patient in a mental institution, or have you ever been treated for a mental illness?.................☐ Yes ☐ No

(11) Are deportation proceedings pending against you, or have you ever been deported or ordered deported, or have you ever applied for suspension of deportation or for preexamination?..☐ Yes ☐ No

(12) Do you owe any Federal taxes?..☐ Yes ☐ No

State last year for which you filed a Federal income tax return.........

(13) Have you ever represented yourself to be a United States citizen?...☐ Yes ☐ No

(14) *(a)* Have you ever deserted from the military, air, or naval forces of the United States?...............................☐ Yes ☐ No

    (b) If male, have you ever left the United States to avoid being drafted into the Armed Forces of the United States?........☐ Yes ☐ No

(15) The law provides that you may not be regarded as qualified for naturalization, if, at *any* time during the period for which you are required to prove good moral character, you believed in polygamy or have been a polygamist; have received most of your income from illegal gambling; have committed adultery; have been a prostitute or have procured anyone for prostitution; or have been a drug addict or have dealt illegally in drugs. Have you *ever, anywhere*, been such a person or committed any of these acts?.........☐ Yes ☐ No

(16) Do you believe in the U.S. Constitution and form of Government of the United States?.................................☐ Yes ☐ No

(17) Are you willing to take the full oath of allegiance to the United States? (See Instructions).........................☐ Yes ☐ No

(18) If the law requires it, are you willing:

    (a) to bear arms on behalf of the United States?..☐ Yes ☐ No

    (b) to perform noncombatant services in the Armed Forces of the United States?.....................................☐ Yes ☐ No

    (c) to perform work of national importance under civilian direction?..☐ Yes ☐ No

(19) *(a)* If male, did you ever register under United States Selective Service laws or draft laws?.........................☐ Yes ☐ No

    If "Yes" give date ....; Selective Service No.................; Local Board No..........; Present classification............

    (b) Were you ever exempted from service because of conscientious objections, alienage, or other reasons?................☐ Yes ☐ No

    If "Yes," state reasons ....

(20) If serving or ever served in the Armed Forces of the United States, give branch...;

from................., 19 .... to ...., 19 ...., and from................, 19 .... to ...., 19....;

☐ inducted or ☐ enlisted at...; Service No...........................;

type of discharge...; rank at discharge...;
           (Honorable, Dishonorable, etc.)

reason for discharge...
                        (alienage, conscientious objector, other)

☐ Reserve or ☐ National Guard from..19.....to.....

STATEMENT OF FACTS FOR PREPARATION OF PETITION
SECTION OF LAW ....

```
┌─────────────────────────────────────────────┐
│              ALIEN REGISTRATION              │
│  Name ....................................... │
│  No. ........................................ │
└─────────────────────────────────────────────┘
```

(1) My full, true, and correct name is ....
(Full, true name, without abbreviations)

(2) My present place of residence is ....
(Number and street)   (City or town)   (County)   (State)

(3) I was born on .... in ....
(Month)   (Day)   (Year)   (City or town)   (County, district, province, or State)   (Country)

(4) I am .... and have .... living children. The first name of my husband or wife is (was) .... ;
(Single; married; divorced; widowed)

we were married on .... at .... ;
(Month)   (Day)   (Year)   (City or town)   (State or country)

he or she was born at ....
(City or town)   (County, district, province, or State)   (Country)

on .... ; entered the United States at ....
(Month)   (Day)   (Year)   (City or town)

.... on .... for permanent residence in the United States and
(State)   (Month)   (Day)   (Year)
☐ with me
now resides ☐ apart from me at .... ;
(Show full address if not living with you)

and was naturalized on .... at ....
(Month)   (Day)   (Year)   (City or town)   (State)

Certificate No. .... or became a citizen by ....
....

(5) I was lawfully admitted to the United States for permanent residence on .... ;
(Month)   (Day)   (Year)

under the name of .... at ....
(City)   (State)

on the ....
(Name of vessel or other means of conveyance)

(6) I have resided continuously in the United States of America since .... and continuously in the
State of .... where I now live since .... and during the past
5 years I have been physically present in the United States for an aggregate period of .... months.

(7) I (have, have not) previously filed petition for naturalization No. .... on ....
(Month)   (Day)   (Year)

at .... in the .... Court.
(City)   (State)

(8) I wish the naturalization court to change my name to ....
(Give full name desired or state "None")

(9) Since such lawful admission, I have not been absent from the United States *for a period or periods of 6 months or longer* except as follows
(if none, state "None"):

DEPARTED FROM THE UNITED STATES			RETURNED TO THE UNITED STATES		
PORT	DATE (Month, day, year)	VESSEL OR OTHER MEANS OF CONVEYANCE	PORT	DATE (Month, day, year)	VESSEL OR OTHER MEANS OF CONVEYANCE

(10) My children now living are: (Complete all columns as to each child. If child lives with you, state "with me" in last column; otherwise,
give city and state of child's residence.)

NAME	SEX	PLACE BORN	DATE BORN	NOW LIVING AT—

4

(11) Do you intend to reside permanently in the United States? ....☐ Yes ☐ No
If "No," explain: ....
(12) My last place of foreign residence was ....
(City)   (Country)

(13) My father's full name is ....
(14) My mother's maiden name was ....
(15) I came to the United States from the port of ....
(City)   (Country)

(16) The person in the United States to whom I was coming was ....
(17) The place in the United States to which I was going was ....
(18) The names of some of the passengers or other persons I traveled with, including members of my own family and their relationship to me, if any, were ....
....

Signature of person preparing form, if other than applicant.	SIGNATURE OF APPLICANT
I declare that this document was prepared by me at the request of applicant and is based on all information of which I have any knowledge. SIGNATURE	
	ADDRESS AT WHICH APPLICANT RECEIVES MAIL
ADDRESS: DATE:	

TO APPLICANT: DO NOT FILL IN BLANKS BELOW THIS LINE.

NOTE CAREFULLY.—This application must be sworn to before an officer of the Immigration and Naturalization Service at the time you appear before such officer for examination on this application.

AFFIDAVIT

I do swear that I know the contents of this application comprising pages 1 to 4, inclusive, and the supplemental forms thereto, No(s). ...., subscribed to by me; that the same are true to the best of my knowledge and belief; that corrections numbered ( ) to ( ) were made by me or at my request; and that this application was signed by me with my full, true, and correct name, SO HELP ME GOD.

Subscribed and sworn to before me by applicant at the preliminary investigation ( ) at ....
this .... day of ...., 19 ......
I certify that before verification the above applicant stated in my presence that he had (heard) read the foregoing application, corrections therein and supplemental form(s) and understood the contents thereof.

(Complete and true signature of applicant)

(Naturalization examiner)

(For demonstration of applicant's ability to write) ....

(1st witness) ....Occupation ....
residing at ....
(Street address, city or town, and State)

(2d witness) ....Occupation ....
residing at ....
(Street address, city or town, and State)

U.S. .... State .... Physical presence .... mos. ....
(Naturalization examiner)

ARRIVAL RECORD FOUND	ARRIVAL RECORDS EXAMINED
Place	Card index ....
Name	Index books ....
.... Age	Manifests ....
Date .... Marital status	
Manner	(Signature of person making search)

Nonfiled ....
(Dates, reasons, and examiner's initials)

INSTRUCTIONS TO THE APPLICANT
(Tear off this instruction sheet before filling out this form.)

You must be at least 18 years old to file a petition for naturalization. Using ink or a typewriter, answer every item in the application form whether you are male or female. UNLESS YOU ANSWER ALL ITEMS IN FULL, IT MAY BE NECESSARY TO RETURN THE APPLICATION TO YOU. IF YOU DO NOT HAVE ENOUGH SPACE TO ANSWER A QUESTION COMPLETELY, ADD THE WORD "CONTINUED" AFTER THE ANSWER IN THE APPLICATION, THEN FINISH YOUR ANSWER ON A SEPARATE SHEET OF PAPER THIS SIZE, AND SHOW ON THAT PAPER THE NUMBER OF THE QUESTION(S) YOU ARE ANSWERING, YOUR NAME, AND YOUR ALIEN REGISTRATION NUMBER.

APPLICATIONS SUBMITTED BY RELATIVES.—If you desire to be called for examination at the same time as another member of your family who is also submitting an application to file a petition for naturalization, please indicate this desire on a separate sheet of paper, attached to this application, showing the name and file number of the relative(s).

YOU MUST SEND WITH THIS APPLICATION THE FOLLOWING THREE THINGS:

1. PHOTOGRAPHS.—THREE IDENTICAL PHOTOGRAPHS of yourself taken within 30 days of the date of this application. THESE PHOTOGRAPHS MUST BE 2 BY 2 INCHES IN SIZE. NO OTHER SIZE SHOULD BE SUBMITTED. The distance from the top of the head to the point of the chin should be approximately 1¼ inches. They must not be pasted on a card or mounted in any other way, must be on thin paper, must have a light background, and must clearly show a front view of your face without hat. They may be in natural color or in black and white, but black and white photographs which have been tinted or otherwise colored are not acceptable. DO NOT SIGN YOUR PHOTOGRAPHS. Using soft lead pencil to avoid mutilation of photographs, write your ALIEN REGISTRATION number lightly on the reverse of photographs, making sure that you place it in the center, away from the edges of the photographs.

2. FINGERPRINT CHART.—A RECORD OF YOUR FINGERPRINTS, taken on the fingerprint chart furnished you with this application. Write in your Alien Registration number on the chart in the space marked "Number," then take it with these instructions to any police station, sheriff's office, or office of the Immigration and Naturalization Service for fingerprinting. You must then sign the chart in the presence of the officer taking the fingerprints, and have him sign his name and title and fill in the date in the spaces provided. DO NOT BEND, FOLD, OR CREASE THE FINGERPRINT CHART.

3. BIOGRAPHIC INFORMATION.—You must complete every item in the Biographic Information form furnished you with this application, and sign your name on the line provided.

ALIEN REGISTRATION RECEIPT CARD.—DO NOT SEND your Alien Registration Receipt Card with this application.

DATE OF YOUR ARRIVAL.—If you do not know the exact date of your arrival in the United States, or the name of the vessel or port, give the facts as well as you remember them or are able to get them. If the date of your arrival in the United States was before June 30, 1906, you should submit with this application any documents you may have to show that you have been living in the United States since before that date such as family Bible entries, deeds, leases, wills, life insurance policies, bankbooks, employment records, receipts, and school records.

(SEE OVER)

EXAMINATION ON GOVERNMENT AND LITERACY.—Every person applying for naturalization must show that he or she has a knowledge and understanding of the history, principles, and form of Government of the United States. There is no exemption from this requirement, and you will therefore be examined on these subjects when you appear before the examiner with your witnesses.

You will also be examined on your ability to read, write, and speak simple English. An exemption from this part of the examination is allowed only for persons who are physically unable to meet these requirements, and for persons who had lived in the United States for as much as 20 years before December 24, 1952, and had already reached 50 years of age by that date.

OATH OF ALLEGIANCE.—You will be required to take the following oath or affirmation of allegiance to the United States in order to become a citizen including, unless you are excepted by law because of religious training and belief, the promises shown relating to bearing arms and performing noncombatant service when required by law:

I hereby declare, on oath, that I absolutely and entirely renounce and abjure all allegiance and fidelity to any foreign prince, potentate, state or sovereignty, of whom or which I have heretofore been a subject or citizen; that I will support and defend the Constitution and laws of the United States of America against all enemies, foreign and domestic; that I will bear true faith and allegiance to the same; that I will bear arms on behalf of the United States when required by the law; that I will perform noncombatant service in the armed forces of the United States when required by the law; that I will perform work of national importance under civilian direction when required by the law; and that I take this obligation freely without any mental reservation or purpose of evasion; so help me God.

"Religious training and belief" means a person's belief in a relation to a Supreme Being involving duties superior to those arising from any human relation, but does not include essentially political, sociological, or philosophical views or a merely personal moral code.

U.S. GOVERNMENT PRINTING OFFICE : 1967 OF—249-929

INSTRUCTIONS: Use typewriter. Be sure all copies are legible and complete. DO NOT REMOVE CARBONS. Failure to comply with instructions delays action. If typewriter is not available, print heavily in block letters with ball-point pen.

★ U S GOVERNMENT PRINTING OFFICE 1967 274-657

FORM G-325 A REV 4-1-67

FORM APPROVED
BUDGET BUREAU NO 43-R436

BIOGRAPHIC INFORMATION

UNITED STATES DEPARTMENT OF JUSTICE
Immigration and Naturalization Service

(FAMILY NAME)	(FIRST NAME)	(MIDDLE NAME)	☐ MALE ☐ FEMALE	BIRTHDATE (MO-DAY-YR.)	NATIONALITY	ALIEN REGISTRATION NO. (IF ANY)

ALL OTHER NAMES USED	CITY AND COUNTRY OF BIRTH	SOCIAL SECURITY NO (IF ANY)

	FAMILY NAME	FIRST NAME	DATE, CITY AND COUNTRY OF BIRTH (IF KNOWN)	CITY AND COUNTRY OF RESIDENCE
FATHER				
MOTHER (MAIDEN NAME)				

SPOUSE (IF NONE, SO STATE) FAMILY NAME (FOR WIFE, GIVE MAIDEN NAME)	FIRST NAME	BIRTHDATE	CITY & COUNTRY OF BIRTH	DATE OF MARRIAGE	PLACE OF MARRIAGE

FORMER SPOUSES (IF NONE, SO STATE)

FAMILY NAME (FOR WIFE, GIVE MAIDEN NAME)	FIRST NAME	BIRTHDATE	DATE & PLACE OF MARRIAGE	DATE AND PLACE OF TERMINATION OF MARRIAGE

APPLICANT'S RESIDENCE LAST FIVE YEARS. LIST PRESENT ADDRESS FIRST.

STREET AND NUMBER	CITY	PROVINCE OR STATE	COUNTRY	FROM MONTH	FROM YEAR	TO MONTH	TO YEAR
						PRESENT TIME	

LAST FOREIGN RESIDENCE OF MORE THAN ONE YEAR IF NOT SHOWN ABOVE. (INCLUDE ALL INFORMATION REQUESTED ABOVE.)

APPLICANT'S EMPLOYMENT LAST FIVE YEARS. (IF NONE, SO STATE) LIST PRESENT EMPLOYMENT FIRST.

FULL NAME AND ADDRESS OF EMPLOYER	OCCUPATION	FROM MONTH	FROM YEAR	TO MONTH	TO YEAR
				PRESENT TIME	

LAST OCCUPATION ABROAD IF NOT SHOWN ABOVE. (INCLUDE ALL INFORMATION REQUESTED ABOVE.)

THIS FORM IS SUBMITTED IN CONNECTION WITH APPLICATION FOR: ☐ NATURALIZATION ☐ ADJUSTMENT OF STATUS ☐ OTHER (SPECIFY):	IF YOUR NATIVE ALPHABET IS IN OTHER THAN ROMAN LETTERS, WRITE YOUR NAME IN YOUR NATIVE ALPHABET IN THIS SPACE:
PENALTIES: SEVERE PENALTIES ARE PROVIDED BY LAW FOR KNOWINGLY AND WILLFULLY FALSIFYING OR CONCEALING A MATERIAL FACT.	DATE _____ (SIGNATURE OF APPLICANT OR PETITIONER)

APPLICANT:

BE SURE TO PUT YOUR NAME AND ALIEN REGISTRATION NUMBER IN THE BOX OUTLINED BY HEAVY BORDER BELOW.

COMPLETE THIS BOX (FAMILY NAME)	(GIVEN NAME)	(MIDDLE NAME)	(ALIEN REGISTRATION NUMBER)

(OTHER AGENCY USE)	(INS USE)

(1) Ident.

FORM G-325A

FEDERAL BUREAU OF INVESTIGATION
UNITED STATES DEPARTMENT OF JUSTICE
WASHINGTON, D.C. 20537

APPLICANT

To obtain classifiable fingerprints:

1. Use printer's ink.
2. Distribute ink evenly on inking slab.
3. Wash and dry fingers thoroughly.
4. Roll fingers from nail to nail, and avoid allowing fingers to slip.
5. Be sure impressions are recorded in correct order.
6. If an amputation or deformity makes it impossible to print a finger, make a notation to that effect in the individual finger block.
7. If some physical condition makes it impossible to obtain perfect impressions, submit the best that can be obtained with a memo stapled to the card explaining the circumstances.
8. Examine the completed prints to see if they can be classified, bearing in mind the following:

Most fingerprints fall into the patterns shown below (other patterns occur infrequently and are not shown here):

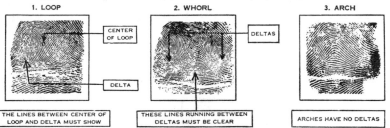

1. LOOP	2. WHORL	3. ARCH
CENTER OF LOOP / DELTA	DELTAS	
THE LINES BETWEEN CENTER OF LOOP AND DELTA MUST SHOW	THESE LINES RUNNING BETWEEN DELTAS MUST BE CLEAR	ARCHES HAVE NO DELTAS

Law-enforcement agencies using this card for pistol permits, licenses, etc., should indicate type of permit or position in space "COMPANY AND ADDRESS."

Department of Defense activities and contractors initiating this card will make no entries in "CONTRIBUTOR AND ADDRESS" and "NUMBER." Such entries will be made by the Department of Defense investigative agencies concerned. Department of Defense activities using this card for military personnel or civilian employees will enter designation and address of requesting activity in "COMPANY AND ADDRESS." Department of Defense contractors will enter contractor's name and address in "COMPANY AND ADDRESS."

The space "NUMBER" should contain the number designated for the particular case or code designation. The number appearing in this space will be quoted on answers to the fingerprint sea?

FD-258
(REV. 9-27-65)

APPLICANT

LEAVE THIS SPACE BLANK	LAST NAME	FIRST NAME	MIDDLE NAME	SEX	RACE

SIGNATURE OF PERSON FINGERPRINTED | CONTRIBUTOR AND ADDRESS — USINS | COMPANY AND ADDRESS | HT. (Inches) WT. | HAIR EYES

RESIDENCE OF PERSON FINGERPRINTED | CITY & STATE | DATE OF BIRTH

NUMBER | LEAVE THIS SPACE BLANK

SIGNATURE OF OFFICIAL TAKING FINGERPRINTS | DATE FINGERPRINTED | CLASS. _____

PLACE OF BIRTH

TYPE OR PRINT ALL REQUESTED DATA | REF. _____

See reverse side for further instructions | CITIZENSHIP

1. RIGHT THUMB	2. RIGHT INDEX	3. RIGHT MIDDLE	4. RIGHT RING	5. RIGHT LITTLE

6. LEFT THUMB	7. LEFT INDEX	8. LEFT MIDDLE	9. LEFT RING	10. LEFT LITTLE

LEFT FOUR FINGERS TAKEN SIMULTANEOUSLY	LEFT THUMB	RIGHT THUMB	RIGHT FOUR FINGERS TAKEN SIMULTANEOUSLY